# THE MIRACLE OF GOD

Angela Brown

The Miracle of God
www.themiracleofgod.com
Copyright © 2020 Angela Brown

ISBN: 978-1-77277-344-6

All rights reserved. No portion of this book may be reproduced mechanically, electronically, or by any other means, including photocopying, without permission of the publisher or author except in the case of brief quotations embodied in critical articles and reviews. It is illegal to copy this book, post it to a website, or distribute it by any other means without permission from the publisher or author.

Limits of Liability and Disclaimer of Warranty
The author and publisher shall not be liable for your misuse of the enclosed material. This book is strictly for informational and educational purposes only.

Warning – Disclaimer
The purpose of this book is to educate and entertain. The author and/or publisher do not guarantee that anyone following these techniques, suggestions, tips, ideas, or strategies will become successful. The author and/or publisher shall have neither liability nor responsibility to anyone with respect to any loss or damage caused, or alleged to be caused, directly or indirectly by the information contained in this book.

Medical Disclaimer
The medical or health information in this book is provided as an information resource only and is not to be used or relied on for any diagnostic or treatment purposes. This information is not intended to be patient education, does not create any patient-physician relationship, and should not be used as a substitute for professional diagnosis and treatment.

Publisher
10-10-10 Publishing
Markham, ON
Canada

Printed in Canada and the United States of America

# Table of Contents

| | |
|---|---|
| Foreword | v |
| Acknowledgements | vii |
| Chapter 1: A Strong Family | 1 |
| Chapter 2: Who Am I? | 9 |
| Chapter 3: Rollercoaster | 21 |
| Chapter 4: Rebirth | 33 |
| Chapter 5: Tragedy | 43 |
| Chapter 6: Misdiagnosis | 53 |
| Chapter 7: God's Plan | 63 |
| Chapter 8: My Message | 73 |
| Part I: Thrive, Not Just Survive | 73 |
| Part II: Follow Your Dreams | 79 |
| Chapter 9: Resources | 81 |
| Post-Traumatic Stress Disorder (PTSD) | 81 |
| Fibromyalgia (FMS or Fibro) | 83 |
| Chronic Pain Syndrome (CPS) | 85 |
| Type 2 Diabetes | 87 |
| Asthma | 89 |
| Kidney Disease | 91 |
| Work Cited Page | 93 |

# FOREWORD

I first met Angela Brown when she attended one of my speaker training workshops. When she stood up to introduce herself, I immediately took notice of how posed and confident she was. When she said she had just released a book written by twelve women, including herself, I was intrigued. When she told me about the memoir she was writing, I wanted to help her.

Angela is an incredible, brave and courageous woman, having overcome all the obstacles she has had to deal with all her life. Now, Angela wants to use her life experiences to empower you to live your life beyond your circumstances, whether they pertain to a medical diagnosis, or financial or family struggles.

Angela has been through it all, but she still stands strong to face any challenges that may be waiting. Angela says her faith in God has helped her in difficult times. She gives all the praise to God.

After reading *The Miracle of God*, you will see your life in a different way. I'm so proud to be Angela's friend and to be a part of her journey.

**Raymond Aaron**
**New York Times Bestselling Author**

# ACKNOWLEDGEMENTS

I would first like to thank my mom, G. Josephine Thomas, for not only giving birth to me but for being there for my many surgeries. You were my rock when I was at Sick Kids' hospital. I saw children who had been abandoned by their parents and family, even at a young age, and it was heartbreaking to see. But I never worried about you, because I knew you would always come back for me. No matter where I was, Canada or Jamaica, I always knew you were there for me, just a phone call away. I love you so much.

I would like to thank my daughter, Natasha. You were my miracle baby, and you've literally saved my life on many occasions. You've always been there for me and have always been my number one supporter. If not for you continually encouraging me, I would not have written this book. I love you so much, more than words can say.

I would like to thank my sister, Suzette. You have been there my whole life, taking care of me and always trying to protect me, even when I didn't want you to. We sometimes drive each other nuts, but the one thing that's constant is that we love each other. I don't know where I would be without a sister like you. I love you more than words can say.

Thank you to my best friend, Ivita Eastmond. I believe that it was destiny that we met at Miracle Mart so many years ago. You have been like a sister to me. You were there for me, through surgeries, my marriage, and my divorce. You are the best godmother to Natasha and my niece, Leianne. You should win the godmother of the year award. I don't know what I would have done if I didn't have you in my life.

## The Miracle of God

Thank you for giving me my godson, Seth, who is like a son to me. I love you so much.

I would like to thank my brother, Miguel (aka Junior). I have loved you since the first day you were born. I loved having you as my little brother; at times, you were like my son. I know we were apart for a few years, but I missed you so much, and I'm so glad we reconnected. Thank you for giving me my nephew, Alexander (aka Alex).

Thank you to my nieces, Janielle and Leianne, and my nephew, Alex. I love all of you so much. I love you guys like my own children. Thank you, Leianne, for my grandniece, Yara. She has brought so much joy to our family.

Thank you to my family members who are no longer with us: My grandmother, Ethlyn Dayes, you were like a mother to me, and I love you; my sweet, beautiful sister, Kareena, I miss you and love you so much; Miguel George Thomas, thank you for being a good stepfather to me, and I love you. I look forward to seeing you all in heaven someday.

I would like to thank my ex-husband, Nathaniel Brown, for giving me Natasha. She is the love of my life, and without you, I wouldn't have her. Thank you for the years of our marriage when we were happy.

I would like to thank my son-in-law to be, Jonathan Nhau, for making my daughter, Natasha, happy. If you continue to make her happy, you will always be a part of my family. (P.S. I'm looking for some grandkids in a couple of years!) I love you.

I want to say thank you to Leon Hamilton for making my niece, Leianne, happy, and for giving me my grandniece, Yara. Also, thank you to your mom, Cheril Sewell, and family as well, for making us feel welcomed at Christmas and other occasions.

## Acknowledgements

Thank you to Sandra McGee. You are more than Alex's mom; you are a friend, and I love you.

Thank you to Wendell Guy Mckoy for being my brother-in-law. When I had the chicken pox, and no one wanted to go near me, you took care of me. You gave me my two beautiful nieces, and you were a great brother-in-law, protector, caretaker, and friend.

I would like to say thank you to Paul McNaught, for taking care of my best friend, Ivita. Thank you for giving me my godson, Seth.

I would like to say thank you to Dawn Peat-Martin for being a good friend. Also, thank you for giving me my goddaughters, Shaniece and Ashley.

Thank you to Shaniece and Ashley Allan. You are both more than goddaughters; you are like daughters to me, and I love you both so much.

Thank you to my boyfriend, Kevin Marshall. You are a godsend to me. Thank you for being a good support and friend to me. I know we have a great future together, and I can't wait to spend it with you.

Thank you to Kevin's sister, brother and wife, nephews, niece, brother-in-law, and other family members for treating me like a member of the family.

Also, thank you to Kevin's cousins; Candace Philander and Tabitha Liburd.

Thank you to Lisa Farrell and M.K. Piatowski, who were my best friends in high school. I'm so glad we are still friends after all these years. Also, thank you to Darina Quinn. I hope we will reconnect one day!

*The Miracle of God*

Thank you to Joana Pierre and her children for always welcoming us as part of their family. (Special thanks to her daughter, Janna, my unofficial goddaughter; I love you lots.)

Thank you to all the church members at Toronto Church of Christ (TCC), and special thanks to:  Andrew and Suzette Lewis; Yvonne and Michael Richards; Lillian and Richard Hislop; Maria and Gary Williams, and their sweet daughter, Nariyah Williams; Nellie-Baron Michel; Careen Pharell; Jeanette and Micheal Green; Grace Richards; Linda Blaschek; Lisa Richards; Candace Richards; Nicole and Garth Devignes; Ashley and Min-na Hockenberry; Andrea Thomas; George and Gayleen Watts; George-Ann Watts; Vivien Foster;  Zenovia and Darrell Shaw; M. Angela Brown (my twin from another mother); Abigail, Rita, and Albert Laulman; Marcia Peart; and Donna-Mae and Brian Griffiths. You have all been there for me at different times in my life, and I can't say thank you enough to each of you for being my friend. Thank you to all other members of TCC, for being my sisters and brothers in Christ.

Thank you to Jackie Brown for making me believe that writing a book was possible.

Thank you to Uchechi Ezurike-Bosse for giving me the opportunity to write a chapter in *The Courage to Change*.

Thank you to the other authors of *The Courage to Change*: Cheryl Roberts, Tracy Turberfield, Julie Barr, Barb Takeda, Joya Williams-Murray, Lynn Milne, Danielle Hines, M.J. Wilson, Sherry Corbitt, Shandel Shand, and Erin Rodgers (Rochon), and to our editor, Danielle Scruton. I'm so happy I had the opportunity to share this journey with you.

Thank you to my daughter's friends, who are like my own children: Janessa Allan, Jade Powell, Shanae Smith, LeShaunda Gray, Kimberly Mills, Lianne Sterling, Tavia Anderson, and Kendra Smith.

## Acknowledgements

Thank you to my friend, Sandra Walfall. Ever since I met you, when Tavia and Natasha were in grade 4, you adopted us into your family. We were always invited to your family barbeques, birthday parties, and more. You were always there for me and Natasha when I was sick and in the hospital. I love you.

Thank you to Claret Smith for being my friend and study partner in college. It's amazing that our daughters would one day meet and be friends too.

I am extremely grateful to Nitz Soriano, Sharina Soriano, and Aristasia Soriano for being great mentors, friends, and colleagues.

I would also like to thank Bobby and Candy Gocool for their leadership and helping us as we grow our business.

Thank you to Romelda Adonis for being a great colleague and friend.

Thank you to Everton Collington for being a wonderful friend even though we are in competing businesses.

I would also like to say thank you to Eli Howell, Beverly Stubbs, Kay Bromfield, and Rich Anthony for being friends with Suzette and me since we all worked at Druxy's over 30 years ago. I love all of you.

I am deeply grateful to my doctors—Dr. Paul O'Brien, Dr. Swan, Dr. Sikaneta, Dr. Khan, and the late Dr. Guha—for the excellent care they always give me. I owe my life to you.

A great thanks to my occupational therapist, Justin Moy. I would not have gotten through the journey without you.

*The Miracle of God*

Thank you to my personal support worker, Andrea Seepaul. You were the best PSW I could ever ask for, along with your daughter, Savannah.

Thank you to Lillian, Saliba, and Lovisa Charbachi for always welcoming me into their home, and for feeding me lots of delicious cultural food.

Thank you to the members of Daily Hope Church, who have become very important to Kevin and me: Aaron and Dana Kerr, Keisha Wilson, Kurt Jones, and all the other members.

I'm grateful to Sarah Gretzinger, who has been coaching me through this process of writing my book.

Thank you to Mia and Andy Torr for always providing excellent advice, and for planning awesome networking events.

Thank you to the members of Scarborough Twilight Rotary Club for embracing me as a member of your Club.

Thank you to Susan Roper. You are truly a good friend; no matter what you are going through in your life, you always take the time to help me if I need you.

Of course, I must extend my deepest gratitude to Raymond Aaron, Waqas Chaudhry, Waqas Ahmed, and the rest of Raymond's staff for their hard work in making this book a reality.

A special thank you to Emma Aaron for her book, *#Success: How Teens Can Create Their Own Brilliant Future*. It was a great model for me to follow as I wrote my book.

A special thank you to Nikki Clarke and Kula Sellathurai for the time they took to give me their testimonials for my book.

# CHAPTER 1

## A STRONG FAMILY

*"Families are like branches on a tree. You grow in different directions, yet your roots remain as one."*
– Unknown

I'm glad we all made the effort to get together, to encourage my mom. It had been a while since everyone had gotten together for a family meal. We are all so busy with our own lives that we skip the family times together. But since today is Family Day, we're all meeting for lunch. Of course, being a West Indian family, agreeing on the time to meet is stressful, and then getting everyone to arrive on time is another story. I can only hope and keep my fingers crossed.

Natasha and I arrived first and were sitting at the table waiting for the rest of the family to arrive. My niece, Janielle, and her dad Wendell (aka Mackie), came in a few minutes later. We all greeted each other with hugs and kisses. Next, Suzette, my mom, and my brother, Miguel, arrived. Of course, Suzette had to change the seating arrangements, which was not surprising at all. We were still waiting for my niece, Leianne, her husband, Leon, and their baby, Yara, the cutest one-year-old ever, to arrive. Leianne is always late—granted, she has a baby to take care of, but she was always late, even before Yara came along.

Natasha and Janielle ordered appetizers to munch on until the latecomers arrived. It wasn't too bad. Leianne was only an hour late;

I'd seen her be later. Once everyone had arrived, it was then time to order, because I was so hungry. It was four o'clock, and we were ordering lunch—I think I called it early dinner.

As we all ate "lunch," I looked at everyone, seeing their journey and how they had all got to where they are today. I was reminded of what a strong family we are together and individually. It doesn't matter what adversities come our way; we always overcome. Let me give you some family history.

Let's start with my grandmother. Even though she is no longer with us, I still consider her the matriarch of the family. She was born and raised in Jamaica. She became a widow at an early age, and her husband left her a business. She became an entrepreneur and, later, a single parent when her daughter (my mom), Girlie, was born. She had another daughter, who died at 6 months old. I can't imagine what she went through. There is nothing worse than losing a child. Her grief was overwhelming, so she sent her daughter (my mom), Girlie, to live with her mother (my great grandmother). At age fourteen, Girlie went back to live with her mother (my grandmother). A few years later, Girlie asked her mom if she could go to the United Kingdom to study nursing, and her mother agreed.

My grandmother was a savvy businesswoman. She was the owner of a restaurant and bar, which is a lot of work. She was an awesome cook. When I was growing up, I saw her teach a lot of young men and some women to cook. She reminded me of Chef Ramsey: If the food was not cooked to her satisfaction, she would yell at them and tell them to "get it together!" Lots of times, she would fire them, and then she would feel sorry for them and hire them back. She had a good heart; she would give away the clothes on her back to help someone in need. She was also very impulsive; for example, she decided to turn her current business into a grocery store, and it was very profitable. She kept a part of the restaurant. I really admired my grandmother.

Next, meet my mom. She goes by Josephine instead of Girlie (who could blame her!). She was born in Jamaica to a single mother, and never knew her father. She never had a father figure in her life and didn't really know much about her mother either. She had been sent away at an early age to live with her grandmother, who was physically abusive to her. (Later, my mom would be physically abusive to her children too.) Then, at seventeen years old, she married the "love of her life," and she had two children by her twenty-first birthday.

Her marriage was not a happy ever after fairy tale. My dad was very abusive to her. After several years of abuse, she left him. Many women stay in an abusive marriage for years and years without leaving. My mom was running from her first husband, for a long time, even when they were in different countries. This explains why she never want to see him or talk about him. The divorce and child custody were done through a lawyer that my mom hired.

My mom has dementia, and it has been so stressful for everyone. We have a routine where we visit her every Friday, and we take her to lunch, do her groceries, and do any other errands she needs us to do. She has been complaining that she's lonely, because she lives by herself. There are lots of activities happening in the independent senior living residence every day, but she attends nothing. She could go to movie night, the knitting club, bingo night, coffee and cookies once a week, and more. She doesn't socialize with anyone, except when she goes to church on Sundays.

Since her dementia is getting worse, she forgets things that used to be second nature to her. For example, she cannot operate her TV, she tries to use the TV remote as a phone, she can't use her cell phone and she doesn't remember how to use the kettle or the microwave. If she tries to cook anything, it ends up being burned or undercooked. So, the three of us must visit her several times per week, to cook for her or bring cooked food. Sometimes she doesn't eat the food because she says it doesn't taste good, but we realized that it's her taste buds.

*The Miracle of God*

She does get a personal support worker for seven hours per week to help with laundry and personal care. Although my mom can be very loving and caring, she can also be short-tempered, and verbally abusive to anyone around her.

Now that I'm an adult, and I understand all the things my mom went through, I can see that repeated the same things that had happened to her, with her own children: abandonment by her mom, verbal and physical abuse, and keeping our biological father a secret. I'm happy that we broke the cycle, with our children. We didn't choose our parents, but we need to leave what happened in the past and love her for doing the best she could with what she had been given. We must remember that the bible says to honor our parents. **"Honor your father and your mother, so that you may live long in the land the Lord your God is giving you."** Exodus 20:12 (NIV)

Meet my sister, Suzette. She and I are total opposites. She was born thirteen months earlier than me, but she acted like my mother. She is very opinionated, fiercely protective, and very controlling. She is stubborn and always wants to be in control of everyone's lives— mostly her daughters, Janielle and Leianne, and Natasha and me. Even though we are all adults, she likes to treat us like her children, and she always must have things her own way. But as much as we all declare our independence, whenever something goes wrong, we all turn to her to fix it. For example, Natasha had an accident with a tow truck. Janielle, Natasha, and I were in the car on our way to Suzette's house. Janielle, of course, called her mom. I don't know how she did it, but she was at the accident scene within ten minutes. Thank God, no one was hurt, even though the lift of the truck shattered the windshield on the driver's side. It was God watching over us that Natasha wasn't hurt. **"I am with you and will watch over you wherever you go, and I will bring you back to this land."**

When Suzette arrived, she immediately took over. Two other tow trucks from the same company showed up too. They offered to tow the car free of charge because the accident was their co-worker's fault. I didn't want them to do the towing, but I didn't have a say. Suzette went into the protective mom and negotiation persona. To make a long story short, Suzette made a deal that got Natasha a newer car with less mileage than the car she had before the accident.

Next, meet my princess, Natasha. She is so much like her aunt: very stubborn, opinionated, and always wants to be in control of other people's lives, especially mine. They drive me nuts! I can never have peace because I'm always arguing with one of them. Incidentally, Natasha and Suzette are also a lot like my mom and grandmother. Natasha is a strong and independent young woman. At age twenty-six, I didn't have the strength that she has, and I know she always has my back.

She is very protective of me, because she worries about my health issues even more than I do. I think the incident when she was nine and found me passed out on the floor, which saved my life from a pulmonary embolism, really scared her. Of course, my passing out on the plane to Cuba, and years later at Yara's (Leianne's daughter) dedication, only made her anxiety worse. She wants to make sure that I don't do anything to jeopardize my health, but I also must live my life. Natasha is also an entrepreneur; she is the co-owner of Sashabeauty, which sells beauty products like eyelashes and wigs. It's hard to believe that she graduated from college with a diploma in public relations, and she is in the insurance business like me.

Now, meet Janielle, my oldest niece is a little like me. She's cool, doesn't like confrontation, and takes things in stride. Janielle is a public speaker and champion for people with dyslexia.

Janielle got into a general program at Seneca. At age 19, one of Janielle's teachers told her that she should be tested for dyslexia, and to her surprise, she was in fact dyslexic. This completely turned her world around. Now she understood why she had to struggle so hard to get good grades. After graduating college, Janielle became a visual display artist, working for Harry Rosen, Saks Fifth Avenue, and TopShop. Janielle decided to take the knowledge she learnt from those high-end stores to open her own business. She is a self-employed wardrobe stylist, and a visual display artist. She knows her worth, and she won't let anybody put her down. She's also a public speaker and champion for people with learning disabilities.

Now, meet Leianne. My niece is our world traveller, teaching in places like South Korea and Dubai, and travelling to places like Indonesia, Europe, and more. Now Leianne is a wonderful mother of one-year-old Yara, who's already sassy and a little diva. She's also a wonderful wife, teacher, and entrepreneur. Shortly after Yara was born, she started her own business, Yarabeanboutique, and is co-host of her podcast, While They Nap (WTN). Leianne is a lot like her mother: opinionated, independent, and always wanting her own way and to be in control.

When I was growing up, my mother didn't want us to have friends. As an only child, she wanted to have lots of children so that they wouldn't have a lonely childhood like she had. She wanted us to be each other's best friend. But when I met Ivita, my mom loved her from the start. She allowed her to move in with our family, and we were "two peas in a pod." We became best friends and more like sisters. It wasn't easy for me to make friends, especially since I was bullied as a child. But when I did, I cherished those friendships, and I still have friends from high school, college, previous employment, and church.

Meet Ivita; she is one of my biggest supporters, and we have known each other for over thirty years. She has overcome some family issues. When we met, she was eighteen years old, and I was twenty-one years old. She changed my life—we went to clubs, on vacation together, and eventually, we moved into a condo as roommates. We fought a lot, but we were always able to put our differences aside. I was upset when Suzette asked her to be Leianne's godmother, because we had always promised to be each other's children's godmother. Looking back now, it was kind of childish. Ivita was the maid-of-honour at my wedding, and she's Natasha's godmother, and my confidant. She is also a wonderful mom to Seth, and I'm his proud godmother. ***"Two are better than one, because they have a good return for their work; if one falls down, his friend can help him up. But pity the man who falls and has no one to help him up!"* Ecclesiastes 4:9-10 (NIV)** never worry about who will pick me up, because I have my family and friends.

Meet Sandra, she's the mother of my nephew Alexander (aka Alex). She and my brother are navigating the ups and downs of co-parenting. Over the years, Sandra and I had a few disagreements over Alex's care, his grades, and other stuff. But deep down, I do think of her as a part of my family.

Let's talk about the men in the family. My brother, Miguel, was the youngest child for both his parents, and he was very spoiled. Growing up, my brother was treated differently from us girls—he didn't do any chores. My stepdad said, "There's enough women in the house to do the chores." They gave him anything he wanted; he got the best brand name clothes and shoes. He got a job at McDonalds when he was younger, but my mom called the manager and cussed him out, and she quit the job for him because the manager made him mop the floor. As a young adult, my brother made some bad decisions. This had a huge impact on his life. He has overcome many set backs, after losing his own father. But he's a great dad to his son.

Finally, meet Alex; he is thirteen. Alex is the comedian of the family; he thinks everything is funny, and it drives me nuts! But I believe that he uses comedy as a coping mechanism to hide his true feelings. From a young age, Alex has pulled a lot of stunts that got him into big trouble. I won't mention what they were because I don't want to embarrass him. He is the only grandson for my mom, and nephew for me and Suzette, so he is spoiled, mostly by his grandmother. He will be going to high school in September 2020. I don't know what the future holds for him, but I know he has a strong family who loves him.

My mom really enjoyed seeing her most of her family together, (Alex couldn't be their because it was short notice and his mom made other plans) getting along and no drama. Now that you have met my family, it's time for you to meet me. I'm ready to share my story with you. Continue reading I know you will be inspired, encouraged, and maybe shocked at some of my stories.

## CHAPTER 2

## WHO AM I?

*"For you created my inmost being,*
*You knit me together in my mother's womb.*
*I praise you because I am fearfully and wonderfully made;*
*Your works are wonderful,*
*I know that full well."*
**Psalms 139:13–14 (NIV)**

Many doctors, nurses, and medical technicians have told me repeatedly that I'm a medical miracle, and that I'm special or rare. They look at me with excitement, expecting me to be excited too. But I've never felt like a medical miracle until December 16, 2012. That night, an incident that may have lasted thirty seconds changed my opinion and my life forever.

My journey began on July 16, 1964, in Huddersfield, UK, where I was born. I had one sister, Suzette, who was one year older than me. I was born premature with several congenital abnormalities, including heart disease. I became a patient from that day on. As I grew up, doctors realized that my health issues were more severe than initially thought.

My mom suffered years of abuse from her husband, who drank and partied too much. After he hit her and broke her nose, she knew that it was time to get out. She told my grandmother what was happening, so the two of them came up with a plan to escape from him. She told him that her mother in Jamaica was very sick, and being the only child, she had to go to Jamaica to take care of her. The plan worked; he took his wife and his two daughters to the airport, kissed them goodbye, and never saw them again. I was two years old and my sister Suzette was three years old.

Soon after, my mom left Jamaica again, without Suzette and me. My grandmother was taking care of three children: my sister, Suzette; Marlene, my cousin; and myself. She was very loving and nurturing. She was obviously a little more protective of me. If anyone ever hurt her grandchildren or niece, they better watch out!

I remember an incident one day where I got a beating with a yardstick, by my kindergarten teacher. We were learning our multiplication tables. Whenever the teacher pointed to someone with the yardstick, the person was expected to answer quickly, and she would keep going around from student to student. We were singing fast, like a song, and we didn't have time to think of the answer; she was drilling it into us. It's not that I didn't know my multiplication tables; I just didn't say it fast enough.

I did get a lot of "licks" on my legs with the yardstick. I could barely walk home; my legs were hurting and burning. We got home late that day, because I had to walk slowly. When my grandmother saw me, she was shocked and very upset. She had already heard what had happened from my cousin, who had walked home ahead of us. The next day, I didn't go to school, but my grandmother did. All I know is that she had a few words for the teacher, especially because she was scared that something bad would happen and make my heart condition worse. I never got any beatings from the teacher again.

I loved living in Jamaica. It was hot most days, and I liked the feeling of the warm sun on my face. I loved fruits, especially the star apples, June plums, soursops, and the sweetness of oranges, mangoes, and sugar cane. But life in Jamaica was so much different than in Canada. When we were younger, my grandmother had maids who gave us a bath, combed our hair, washed our clothes, and made sure we ate. My fondest memory was waking up every Sunday morning to the voice of my grandmother, playing records and singing gospel music. My grandmother was very spiritual, and she wanted us to grow up with the knowledge of God. Every Sunday, we would have a bible study class, and we had to recite a Psalm that she had given us to memorize the previous week. Then she would give us another one to study for the following Sunday. Then we went to church, and the children went to what was referred to as Sunday school. Once Sunday school was over, the children joined the adults in the regular service. The service took so long that I always fell asleep.

Schools in Jamaica were very strict about what the students wore, as well as about hygiene and the presentation of ourselves. For example, we wore uniforms to school, and they had to be clean and pressed every day, and we wore black or brown shoes that needed to be cleaned every day; otherwise, we would be punished. (That could be a whipping.) I liked wearing uniforms because I didn't have to spend unnecessary time in the morning trying to decide what to wear. Most of the schools were divided up with all girls or all boys. I liked this because there was no boy-girl drama or fighting over boyfriends. The flip side was that it made some of us, including me, shy and insecure around boys, even in later years.

I can remember my grandmother taking me to the hospital whenever I had a slight cough or cold. The doctor would give me an injection of antibiotics in the rear end, so it could reach my bloodstream faster than pills. As I grew up, this became a regular routine. My grandmother was always afraid that I would get sicker. Sometimes I tried to hide from her when I wasn't feeling well, but she always knew, so off we went to the hospital.

## The Miracle of God

When I was about seven years old, my grandmother told my sister and I that we would be going to Canada to live with our mom. This was very scary because even though she was our mother, we barely knew her. Now we would be leaving our "mamma" to move to a strange country with someone who was almost a stranger. We had seen her pictures, and she sent us gifts for our birthdays and Christmas too. I have this vision that she had come back to Jamaica once in the middle of the night, and my grandmother woke us up. She brought us lots of clothes and toys, and we were so excited. Then not long after, she would leave again. I still don't know if this really happened or if it was just a dream or fantasy.

We lived in Jamaica with my grandmother, without our mother and father, for many years. I felt like an orphan because our parents were living in different countries from us. I remembered sometimes crying because it was like we had been abandoned by them, especially my father. He never wrote or visited us; it was like we did not exist to him. At least my mom did write, send gifts, and visit, and we did at least know what she looked like. I had a picture of my mother in my head, but I had no idea what my father looked like—he was a dark figure in my dreams. I had so many dreams about him and what he looked like. In my dreams, he would come to Jamaica to visit us and bring us wonderful gifts. But best of all, we would visit him in England. I would be so happy, until I woke up and realized it was just a dream. I spent so many years praying and wishing for him to show up, but it never happened.

On February 28, 1973, my sister and I arrived in Canada. We were warned that it would be cold, but nothing could prepare us for how cold it really was. My mom brought us each sweaters, coats, hats, gloves, scarves, and boots to the airport. But even with all the stuff we had to wear, when we got outside, it was still very, very cold, and I saw smoke coming from our noses and mouths. I had many emotions: I was scared, overwhelmed, and happy to see my mom. I couldn't stop looking at her face to see if it was real or a dream. When we got home, my mom had a big surprise for us. She was a beautiful baby and, at first, I thought it was a doll; she was in a crib drinking a bottle of milk. We soon realized that she was our sister, whom we had not heard about before. I was so excited that I was now a big sister. Her name was Kareena, and she was two years old and so cute—this was a great surprise. I felt so happy and excited to be a big sister.

For the next few days, my mom took us on a tour of our new home, and she bought us clothes and accessories for school, and a few toys. My mom followed the same tradition that the three of us would go to church every Sunday. She would have a bus from a local church come pick us up on Sunday morning. She didn't come with us because she had to work or rest. Of course, we didn't have maids, like in Jamaica, so Suzette and I had to learn to cook, clean, and wash clothes and take care of Kareena. We were in a different world now, with big responsibilities, and if we did not do them, we would get spanked.

A couple weeks after we came to Canada, my mom, Kareena, and I went to The Hospital for Sick Children. I didn't know at the time that this place was going to be my home away from home. We spent the whole day there, doing many tests and seeing many doctors. The initial results were that I was underdeveloped for my age. I was 8 years old, weighed 38 pounds, and was just over 3 feet 6 inches tall. I looked like I had been starved and malnourished. The doctors told my mom that I had 2 holes in my heart, along with valve issues, and a groin hernia, scoliosis (which was a curved spine), strabismus in my right eye, deformity of my left hand pinkie finger, and other congenital defects.

I would need surgery as soon as possible. The doctors also said that they wouldn't be able to repair my heart problems with one surgery, so I would likely have two to three surgeries. My mom was also told that if I had remained in Jamaica for six additional months, I would be dead. I remember a story that Suzette told me: The two of us had gone to the mall, and a lady stopped us and gave my sister money. The lady told her to use the money to buy food for me. She tried to explain that I looked the way I did because I had health issues, not because I was hungry, but the lady didn't believe her, and she insisted we keep the money.

Soon after coming to Canada, I had open heart surgery to repair the two holes. I vaguely remembered the surgeries, but my mom told me that the first surgery took 8 hours. It was performed by a famous cardiac surgeon, Dr. Mustard, at The Hospital for Sick Children, one year before he retired. My mom told me at the time that he was transitioning to spend more time teaching, but she pleaded with him to perform the surgery. I do remember the kind and friendly nurses who took care of me.

I was in the hospital for 2 months, and I received very nice cards from my teacher and classmates. I also received other gifts, like the furry, purple winter coat from my mom's co-workers, and my favourite doll from my mother. Mrs. Beasley came from my favourite TV show, *Family Affair*. I really loved her. She was my best friend, and I told her all my secrets.

I made friends with the nurses, doctors, and other children. The nurses were so nice and caring; we would call them by their names because they felt like family. When I was feeling up to it, I would go to the playroom and play games with the other kids; my favourite game was Trouble. Since there were four kids in a room, there was always someone to play or talk to if we felt like it. Sometimes I just played with Mrs. Beasley or other stuffed animals. We had two TVs in our room, one on each side to share, and they were attached from the ceiling. We had to ask the nurses to turn it off and on, and we all had to watch the same thing. Otherwise, it would be too distracting. We had a lot of fun and laughed with each other.

My mom was not able to visit every day. She had to work and take care of Suzette and Kareena. It was the same for some of the other kid's parents. So, we had to make the best of the situation. We didn't have phones in our rooms; so, when my mom called, I would have to go to the nurse's desk to talk to her but not for a long time. She just wanted to check in to see how I was doing. If I was unable to go to the desk, the nurses would tell me that she called, and that she said, "I love you, and I will visit soon!" It usually worked out that at least one parent would visit, so they became the substitute parent for all the kids in the room.

As part of my daily routine, I would go to school at the hospital. My teachers would send schoolwork for me through Suzette, which I loved doing. I was a straight A student, even though I spent many months away from school. I would get a nice card from my teacher and classmates. I was very confused, because I thought they hated me. When I was at school, no one wanted to play with me; I was always the last one picked for group activities, and I had no friends (unlike Suzette, who was popular and had lots of friends). I figured the teacher probably forced them to make the cards.

When I was released from the hospital, I had a nurse that came to take care of me and Kareena. I had a very big hole in my stomach, between my breast and belly button. It was not covered with gauze or bandages, and the nurse would bathe me and make sure the hole was healing well. I went through a few nurses because my mom would fire them if she wasn't happy with them. For example, one of the nurses gave me a bath in the kitchen sink, because I was so small. When my mom found out, she was livid, and she called the agency and insisted they send a new nurse. When I think back about it now, it seems so funny.

I remembered one place where we lived; our front door locked automatically when it was shut. One day, after my first surgery, Kareena and I were at home with the nurse, and I went outside to get the newspaper (I loved to read the newspaper; my mom said my dad did too). The nurse ran after me because I wasn't supposed to be outside. Kareena was 3 years old; she saw the door opened, and she shut the door and locked us outside. Because of her cognitive delay and her physical limitations, only being able to use her right hand, Kareena was not able to unlock the door to let us back inside the house. I could hear her crying so hard on the other side of the door. After several minutes of coaching her, we realized that she wasn't going to be able to open the door. There was a travel agency located beside us, so the nurse and I went there and asked to use the phone to call my mom. She had to leave work to come home and let us inside the house. As a result of this incident, my mom was fired from her job as a nurse's aide. She decided that she didn't want anyone else taking care of me, so she became my nurse until I was able to go to school.

At home, when I couldn't go to school, I would play school; I would play in my own make-believe world. I would line up my dolls and stuffed animals across my bed and give them names. Then I would teach them to talk; of course, it was my voice, but I tried to make it sound different. I made them walk too. Even though they weren't real, they made me feel good. Since Suzette was at school, and I felt so lonely with no one to talk to, they became my friends too. Sometimes, if she would let me, I would use Kareena as my human pupil. I used my dolls and stuffed animals to create stories about things I wished I had in my life, like my dad. I lived in a fantasy world with my characters. I had hours and hours of fun playing with them. They had a mom and a dad, and siblings. They had the perfect life; I wished so much that could be my life.

When I returned to school, I was not allowed to go outside for recess. The doctors felt that it was safer for me. I spent a lot of time in the library, while the other students went outside for recess or were in gym class. I read a lot and became a librarian helper. I decided that I would be a librarian when I grew up. When my classmates were going to swim class or going on class field trips, I still was not allowed to go. Of course, it made me more of an outcast, and I still had no friends. I did get a surprise, one Christmas after I got out of the hospital. I didn't get to share in any of the special activities that the other children did at school, like Kris Kringle. In the new year, when I returned to school, my teacher gave me a box wrapped with Christmas paper. I was so excited to open it, so I quickly ripped off the paper and opened the box. Inside was a perfume, and it had a strong lemon scent, like lemonade. It was my Kris Kringle gift from a classmate. I never used the perfume, but I kept it for a long time as a reminder that they had thought of me. I missed many more special events at school; oddly enough, I felt more accepted and wanted at the hospital than I did at school.

I hated school—not because of schoolwork but because I was called names and bullied almost every day. I was bullied a lot by boys; I was so shy and introverted, and not used to boys, and I didn't know what to do or say. Truth be told, I loved to study and read. I thought that being in a new country may be different, but it was much worse. I was called names like "dwarf, shrimp, and midget," and a new word I hadn't been called before: "Nigger." This was my first introduction to racism. I was a prime target for bullies, I was constantly picked on, hit, and ridiculed. Suzette was my protector; she would beat up anyone who harassed me. The problem was that she was always in trouble and being sent to the principal's office for fighting. She would get detention even when we tried to explain what happened, and when we got home, Mom would be so mad that she would get a severe spanking.

My mom was protective of her children. If anyone hurt one of her children, she was ready to go to war, which had gotten her into trouble on more than one occasion. One day after school, some kids were ganging up on me on the school bus. As I walked to my building, three girls followed me in the elevator to my floor. They didn't even live in my building; there were three other buildings in a circle. I was so scared, and I didn't know what to do. I wanted to cry, but I didn't give them the satisfaction. Suddenly, one of the girls was pulling my hair, calling me a "nigger," and "Kizzy," from the *Roots* movie that had just come out. Then my mom heard the commotion from inside our apartment, and she opened the door. She saw the three girls following me. She started to scream at them and chased them. The girls ran as fast as they could. When I got in the apartment, I started to cry. She hugged me so tight, and I felt so safe.

Not only did I not have friends at school, I didn't have any in my neighbourhood either. I was very much non-existent. I was sick a lot and not allowed to go out to play. The other problem was that my mom never encouraged us to make friends; she said that we (Kareena, Suzette, and me) could be friends with each other and play together. In this case, Suzette and I were a year apart, so we did like some of the same things, but I was seven years older than Kareena, and she was more delayed than her age. But I did play with her as often as possible.

It seemed like a lifetime ago that I left Jamaica, even though it was less than a year. I missed my grandmother so much; we would talk with her once a week on the phone. My mom would tell her how we were doing, especially about my surgery and what was going to happen next. I knew there were more surgeries to come, but I wasn't worried.

Life settled down into a normal routine. But soon I needed a second surgery. I went through a series of tests before I could have my second surgery. One test that I really hated the most was an angiogram. I remember one time I had this test done, and I was given a light anesthetic, which made me relaxed but not totally asleep, so the doctors were able to talk to me and give me instructions. I felt a sharp pain as the doctor cut my groin. Of course I screamed, and the doctors realized that the freezing of my groin had not numbed the area. I felt a warm sensation as a dye was injected into the catheter. Then I fell asleep. Angiograms became a yearly thing until I was fourteen.

*Who Am I?*

If anyone asks me to describe my childhood, I immediately think of a roller coaster. There were many emotional highs and lows, tight turns, steep slopes, and difficult times. Continue reading to find out why.

.

# CHAPTER 3

# ROLLERCOASTER

*"But when I am afraid, I will put my trust in you."*
**Psalms 56:3 (NIV)**

    These years were challenging for all of us, especially my mom. She was a single mother with three children, and two had major health challenges. As children, we never understood what my mom was going through. She was working two jobs to support us, while dealing with my and Kareena's health issues. She was fired from many jobs because of too many days off. We did many stupid things that contributed to her having to change a lot of jobs.

    Mom knew how much Suzette and I missed our grandmother, so she did her best to make our lives in Canada a happy one. I remember that she got us a parrot, but one day we accidently left the window open, and it flew away. We also had goldfish in a jar, but we would overfeed them, and they died. Since we didn't like going out for Halloween, she would buy us candies so that we wouldn't feel left out from other children. She didn't have a lot of extra money, but we made it work.

    I remember that my mom bought a bicycle for me and Suzette. Of course, since Suzette was bossy and the oldest, she got to use it first. I didn't know how to ride a two-wheel bike, but I was so excited to try. I went outside and got on the bike. I fell off a few times and then I had one last fall—I had bruises on my knees, arms, and legs, and my mom was very upset. The next time we wanted to ride the bicycle, we found out that my mom had sold it, because she didn't want me to get hurt again. I felt bad that Suzette was deprived of some privileges because of me.

In 1974, my mom met someone who she later married, and he became our father. He was the only father figure we ever had. This was a blessing for my mom because she didn't have to take care of three children on her own. She no longer had to work two jobs to make ends meet, while dealing with my and Kareena's health issues. I do remember that he was at the hospital for my second heart surgery, which gave my mom some support.

Losing her firstborn child, a son, affected my mom for many years. When she married my stepdad, she was determined to have a son. She suffered many miscarriages but never gave up on wanting a son. With one of her pregnancies, she had a premature baby girl. They named her Marjorie; but unfortunately, she died after three weeks. The doctor said that my mom should have her tubes tied, but she refused. When my mom got pregnant again, she was on total bedrest for most of her pregnancy, and in the hospital for the two months before she gave birth to my brother by C-section. The doctor and my stepdad persuaded my mom to have her tubes tied before she left the hospital. Years later, she said she regretted that decision. In 1979, my mom had a baby boy, named after his father, and we called him Junior. He was also premature; he was born when my mom was 28 weeks pregnant. He spent a few weeks in the hospital, so my mom and stepdad would have to go to the hospital every day for his feedings. My mom would stay all day, and my stepdad would go to work. Junior also had some health challenges, but after a few years, he fully recovered. Junior was her pride and joy. I believe my mom was finally happy and at peace after she had Junior.

When I was fourteen years old, my parents decided that they were tired of life in Canada, so we moved to Jamaica. We arrived in Jamaica on October 26, 1978. Since my grandmother was well off, it seemed like a good idea at the time. She was getting older in age and needed help to manage her business. My mother and my grandmother had a difficult relationship. This did not change when we moved to Jamaica. They had a lot of unresolved issues, which affected everyone around them. Seeing my mother and grandmother interact together gave me some new information about their lives: They had a very dysfunctional relationship, and they fought a lot about things that had happened in the past when my mom was younger.

I realized that these incidents in my mom's life had an impact on the type of parent she had become. I never had any doubt that my mother loved her children; however, at times, she could be very cold, and verbally and physically abusive to me and my sisters. The fact that we had no biological father in our lives was used to verbally assault us, and we were less worthy because we didn't have a father. My mom never said a kind word about my biological father. She said that he was no good, and that he was a drug addict, an alcoholic, and a cheater. She also said that he physically abused her (she said he broke her nose). I do not disbelieve my mom's version of her marriage to my father, but since I've never had the opportunity to talk to him, I only have one side of the story, and her accounts are prejudiced by her resentment of him. My mother and grandmother conspired together to keep my father away from me and Suzette.

We received gifts from him twice in our lives: winter clothes on one occasion, and 2 watches a few years later. Suzette wrote to him when I was having my first heart surgery but got no response. My mom says that his common-law wife also didn't want us to have a relationship with him, so she may have hidden or thrown out our letters. (Years later, we found out that this was very likely to have happened.) We tried several times to find him, without success. In 1993, I found out that he had died a few months earlier, so we would never get the opportunity to reunite with him. It was very devastating to both of us.

Years later, I found out that my father had a common-law spouse of 30 years. We also found out that he never remarried and never had any more children. I was able to track her down, and we had a three-way conversation, with her, Suzette, and me. This was when we found out how much she resented us. She admitted that she never wanted us to have a relationship with him, and she even burned a letter that he had written to us on his deathbed. I couldn't understand how someone could be so cruel. She spoke about him like she hated him; she was angry because he never wanted to get married again or have any more children.

After two years in Jamaica, my parents decided that it was time to return to Canada, but it would be impossible for them to take all of us at the same time. So they decided to take my brother and leave us girls behind. We didn't care about being left behind again, because my grandmother was like a mother to me and Suzette, and Kareena was happy if we were there. We lived with my grandmother for another year after they left. We were in Jamaica for a total of three years when my mom said that we had to go back to Canada—I cannot say that it was a happy time. We loved living with my grandmother, especially the summer weather, and I had friends. Suzette, who was eighteen years old at the time, was an adult and could make her own decisions. So she decided that she would not return to Canada with us. For her own various reasons, she wanted to stay in Jamaica.

Truth be told, I didn't want to go back either, but I was always the compliant daughter who did what my mom wanted me to do; I never stood up for myself. Also, Kareena, who was eleven years old, could not fly on her own, so I had to go with her. It was the first time in seventeen years that Suzette and I would be apart. We had been together through all the ups and downs. Now I would have to take care of myself, and be Kareena's protector, like Suzette had been to me.

Kareena and I returned to Canada on August 22, 1981. A few months later, my mom took us to HSC for a check-up. It would be my last time going to HSC, because I was seventeen years old. After doing more tests, the doctors told my mom that they found another hole in my heart. My previous surgeries had closed the two holes, but one was remaining. It was so small that the other doctors didn't see it back in 1973. However, they decided that they would not attempt to close the hole. If any problems occurred in the future, then my doctors could make the decision at that time whether to repair it or not. I was warned by the cardiologist that I should not have any children, because my heart may not be able to handle it. I was given my graduation papers from HSC and was transferred to Toronto General Hospital. It was a bittersweet moment. I was so familiar with the doctors and nurses at HSC, and I would really miss them—I was now leaving my second home. I would go to the hospital every five years for check-ups, unless any problems occurred, and then I would go sooner. I am now an adult and am responsible for my own care. My mother did not attend any more check-up appointments with me.

In September 1981, I went to an all-girl catholic high school. I was seventeen years old and was two years behind because of my rollercoaster life between Canada and Jamaica. Being three years older than my classmates made me an outcast. I was also a nerd, and my social interaction skills were very poor. Spending so much of my time in the library in elementary school was a great asset to me. Since Catholic high schools were considered as private, there was a tuition fee, which my mom couldn't afford. I was able to work in the library on my free periods to lower the fee. I also worked part-time after school, which helped with the tuition fee. In grade eleven, I finally made some friends. We would hang out with each other on weekends and during the Christmas and summer breaks. It was hard for me to get close to them and tell them about my life. I never invited them to my house because it just wasn't something we did. They did invite me to their homes to meet their parents and siblings. Their moms were so nice to me, and they treated me like a part of their families. I graduated high school in 1984, at age twenty; I was the oldest in my class. My rollercoaster life had cost me two years of school. I invited my whole family to graduation, and Suzette, Kareena, and my mom and stepdad attended the ceremony and met my friends.

I had my first boyfriend at age eighteen; my mom had set up a meeting with one of her young co-workers. He was very friendly, and we had a lot of fun together. We dated off and on for six years. My family loved him and thought that he was a good match for me. They all saw marriage in our future. But there was one problem: I just didn't see him as "the one." I didn't feel any butterflies when I saw him, or any fireworks when he kissed me. I wanted the fairy tale that I had read about in the Harlequin romance novels, where they find their prince at the end.

When I was eighteen, I got my first job. I should correctly say that my mom got me the job. A few months earlier, my mom had gone with Suzette to the Eaton Center in downtown Toronto to fill out job applications, and she got a job at a fast food restaurant. Once Suzette was settled in the job, my mom got Suzette to ask if they would hire me. It so happened that the manager said yes, so I went to the store to meet him. He was visibly shocked. He was young, handsome, British, and about 6.6 feet tall, and I was about 4.6 feet—he thought I was a little kid. Suzette and I were totally opposites in every way, so he was very stunned; he wasn't expecting *me*. He gave me the challenge that if I could reach the countertop and see the customers, he would hire me. I rose to the challenge and he hired me, and I worked there for almost three years while in high school and college.

I started going to school at Centennial College in Toronto, studying to become a legal assistant. My first day of college was a lot different than I expected. My high school years were surrounded by girls, since it was an all-girls school. I didn't have many opportunities to meet boys, but I was happy about that because boys had been so mean to me in elementary school. Now I was in college, and there were boys.

My first day of college, I was so overwhelmed; the school was so big, and I had to learn to navigate this all by myself. I was rushing because I didn't want to be late for my first class. As I opened the door, I saw many faces staring at me—they were all boys. I took a deep breath; I could feel my knees shaking, and my books were so heavy that I thought they were going to fall. I asked the teacher which class it was, and he said *engineering*. I asked where I could find class xxx, and he told me that it was across the hall. I said thank you, and I closed the door. That was very embarrassing, but I couldn't dwell on it because I still needed to get to my class.

At first, college was very hard for me. I would describe it as feeling like "a fish out of water." My grades were not as good as they were in high school. I worked my butt off to keep up with the reading and homework assignments. My average was in the 60's—all C's. I saw myself as a failure, because I didn't want anything less than a B average. In my second semester, I changed a subject to Accounting and Financial Management. In grade 11, I had taken accounting, and I got great marks in it, so I thought I should pursue it. In order to change my major, I had to get my Law teacher to sign off on it. He asked me why I was changing, and I said that it was because my grades were so low. He then told me that I had one of the highest grades in the class; he signed off on it but recommended that I give it another try.

I continued in the accounting field. After two years of attending college full time, I decided to do it on a part time basis. I didn't want to have a huge student loan to pay back. I met a girl named Ivita while I was working part time at Miracle Mart. I was still in college at this time. Ivita and I didn't hit it off right away. I will admit that it was my fault. I was shy, introverted and suspicious of people.

My world was surrounded by the experiences I had in high school. Even though I was a bit apprehensive with Ivita, eventually we became friends. I did one year of part time studies and then I quit college with only one course left to graduate. I did make friends in college too. These girls were very nice, and we had something in common, because we had a few classes together. It was nice to have someone to hang out with at school during spare periods. We exchanged phone numbers and became good friends. I remained friends with some of them even after college.

After college, I got a full-time job as an assistant to the accountant. Ivita also had a full-time job. We both worked for our companies for about a year. Then we quit our jobs and decided to use our savings for a trip to Florida. We had a great time; however, we made one big mistake that almost ended in disaster—we ran out of money. We got swindled by a very smart T-shirt salesman. We didn't even have any money to buy food, so we had to snack a lot on the free complimentary appetizers at the hotel. We also got free breakfast. I must confess, we took some of the breakfast to our room for lunch, and then some appetizers for dinner—it was a great plan!

On December 27, 1989, I woke up feeling so excited—I was going to start a new job. Then the telephone rang, and it was not good news. All excitement drained from my body when I heard my mom screaming. I rushed to her room and saw her crying uncontrollably. Then my stepdad said that my grandmother had died the night before, in her sleep. I was devastated, and everyone was crying; it was no longer a good day. I had to wipe my tears and go to my new job so that I wouldn't get fired. The next few days, everyone was on autopilot; there were lots of tears and lots of laughter as we remembered stories about my grandmother. My mom and Suzette went to Jamaica to plan the funeral. I was very disappointed that I couldn't go too; I also wanted to say goodbye to my grandmother. But someone had to stay behind to help my dad take care of Junior and Kareena. Plus, I had just started my new job, so I couldn't just leave in such a short time. I later found out that I could have gotten bereavement leave, if I had asked.

While still grieving from my grandmother's death, I found out that I had a very large (5cm) uterine fibroid, which needed to be removed. This surgery could be very dangerous because my fibroid was attached to the outside of my uterus. The doctor suggested that I have a hysterectomy, which I disagreed with. I was twenty-six years old and had never had any children; I didn't want to risk the chance of never having a child. (I did not tell him that I had been warned not to have a child.). The doctor agreed to just remove the fibroid. However, I had to sign papers giving permission that in the event that any complication should occur, like excessive bleeding (hemorrhaging), then he could perform a hysterectomy.

While I waited for my surgery, I prayed every day to God to not let them do a hysterectomy. I knew that my grandmother was in heaven watching over me, and that gave me the comfort I needed to trust in the Lord. *"This is the confidence we have in approaching God: that if we ask anything according to his will, he hears us."* **1 John 5:18**

As soon as I woke up from the surgery, I asked if they had done a hysterectomy; the doctor smiled and said no. I was so excited that I wanted to do a happy dance—of course, I was not physically able to do it. I was in the hospital for one week, then home for six weeks to recover. By this time, I was twenty-six and had had four major surgeries. I was determined not to have anymore, but of course, it wasn't up to me.

In the summer of 1991, my best friend, Ivita, and I went to Jamaica on vacation, and to see my parents. They had retired early to return to Jamaica to handle my grandmother's business and estate. While we were in Jamaica, my mother connected me with someone I knew while living with my grandmother. He became one of our tour guides for the remainder of our vacation. We began a long-distance relationship, and we corresponded by mail for about 6 months. Then he came to Canada in November 1991, and we were married in Canada, on May 30, 1992.

Soon after I got married, I decided to get a second opinion on having a baby. It had been ten years since I was given that advice, and I felt it was necessary to be sure. My family doctor, who had been my primary physician for more than eleven years, recommended that I see a cardiologist. He ordered several tests, including a stress test and wearing a Holter monitor for several days. He also recommended that I see a gynecologist because of my previous fibroid surgery. The results were very promising: Both doctors felt that I could have one or two babies, but I would have to deliver by C-section. Six months after getting married, I became pregnant. Unfortunately, I had a miscarriage shortly after. It was a major disappointment, of which we did not tell anyone. Six weeks after my miscarriage, I wanted to try again. My husband felt that it was too risky to try again, but I disagreed with him. After a few discussions, we decided to give it another try. A few weeks later, I was pregnant again. It was a joyous time and a stressful time; our world turned upside down.

When I told Suzette that I was pregnant, she hung up the phone on me and never spoke to me for three months. I knew she was scared and angry that I had put my life in danger, after the warning I had been given. She did not let me explain that I had gotten other opinions. She did eventually come around, and she embraced the fact that she was going to be an aunt. All was good with us. One week after I told my mom that I was pregnant, she came back to Canada. No one knew she was coming; it was a big surprise. The last time I saw her was at my wedding. As much as I loved to see her, I prayed that she wouldn't stay too long. She stayed for eight months, which was a curse and a blessing for me and my husband. We were newlyweds and wanted the time alone before the baby came. But there was no way to send her back, so we had to adjust to it.

I loved my mom, but she made a very tense situation much worse. My mom, sister, and husband were living on pins and needles that something would go wrong. The worst part of my pregnancy was that I had morning sickness every day, after every meal. I also had doctors' appointments every week. I was either visiting my family doctor, the cardiologist, the OBGYN, or having ultrasounds; I had about four to five ultrasounds and lots of blood work over the nine months of my pregnancy. It was also stressful because my family constantly nagged me to stop working and to take early maternity leave. They also monitored everything I did. I had problems gaining weight in my pregnancy because I vomited after every meal, and I was becoming scared to eat. Eventually, I only ate soup and porridge, as that was all my stomach could tolerate. By the end of my pregnancy, I had broken the blood vessels in both my eyes from vomiting so much. I gained eleven pounds throughout my pregnancy.

When I was a child, my mom asked me, "What do you want to be when you grow up?" My answer was, "A housewife." I got a beating for that answer. Having a child was very important to me, and I was literally risking my life so that I could become a mom. On August 26, 1993, I gave birth to my miracle baby girl by caesarean section. Natasha Justine Brown was born weighing five pounds eleven ounces. When I saw her, I was so happy. I had done what many doctors had thought was impossible, and she was only two weeks early. After 4 hours, a nurse woke me up to feed Natasha, and I was then informed that she was completely healthy and showed no signs of a heart condition. I made the decision that I would not risk having another child. The pregnancy had not gone as smoothly as I thought, but it was all worth it to have my miracle baby daughter.

Unfortunately, life is full of challenges. We will have happy times and sad times, and lots of new beginnings and interesting things in our paths. Continue reading to find out what new beginnings were out there for me.

# CHAPTER 4

# REBIRTH

*"Therefore, if anyone is in Christ, the new creation has come: The old has gone, the new is here!"*
**2 Corinthians 5:17 (NIV)**

On February 19, 1997, I was baptised and became a Christian. When I started to study the bible, I did not intend to get baptised. I already knew a lot about the bible because of my grandmother. After six months, I made the decision to get baptized. When I told my husband, he thought it was too soon, but I disagreed. I asked him to come and support me, and he said he would do it but that I should wait a few months. I got baptised the next day. He was upset that I had not taken his advice, and that I did it without him being there. But I wanted Natasha to grow up knowing about God and the bible, like I did as a child.

Our lives began to drift apart after I got baptised. He was interested in playing cricket, going to parties and bingo, and hanging out in bars with his friends. I was interested in God, Natasha, and my husband. I know that the bible says that the husband must come after God, but Natasha was more important to me than my husband.

I spent a lot of time at church. They had a lot of activities for the adults and the kids. My husband was good about driving us to church, but he didn't come with us. As Natasha learned more about God and got involved in recitals, singing on stage, and other children's activities, she tried to get her dad to come to church. She questioned his reluctance to go to church as a preacher would, even though she was only three years old. It was very hard to see husbands and wives together, both members of the church. I thought if the whole family went to church and worked on the same goals, leading groups and spending more quality time together, it would seem like a perfect family. But of course, everyone knows that there is no "perfect" marriage.

My health remained stable for five years; I had no major health issues, and all was great. Then in 1998, I began to have a problem with my neck. I was having a problem turning my neck, for hours and sometimes days. I also had other symptoms, like extreme pain, numbness and tingling in both hands, and a feeling like electrical shocks—this was called neuropathic pain. It became so severe that I was having problems doing ordinary things like writing, washing dishes, laundry, etc. I was in pain all the time, until I could no longer work. My doctor put me on disability and referred me to a neurologist, which took several months to see her. She recommended that I have an MRI, which took ten weeks. Then she told me that I had something called Short Neck Syndrome, and she was referring me to a neurosurgeon. I waited eight weeks in agony to see the neurosurgeon, who ordered a CAT scan because the MRI was not clear enough. When the results came in, the neurosurgeon said that I had several spinal cord defects: scoliosis, which means that my spine has a sideway S-shape curve; spinal stenosis of lumbar and cervical spine, which is compression of the spinal cord and nerve roots; and I also had degenerative disc disease (DDD).

Then came the news that I didn't want to hear: I would need surgery—a laminectomy and fusion of the cervical spine. This was going to be major surgery and would involve taking bone from my hip to put in my neck. He also warned that I would need to have back surgery once I healed from the neck surgery. The doctor said that I would be able to return to work in six weeks, and the bone in my hip would grow back in twelve weeks. I went home and told my husband, and all I could think about was how we would handle this and make sure Natasha was taken care of. The good news was that it was summer break, so we didn't have to worry about school. I was scared to death. The last thing I wanted was another surgery, but I also wanted the pain to go away so that I could resume a normal life.

On July 9, 1999, I had the laminectomy and fusion surgery on my neck, and the bone was taken from my right hip (Iliac grafting). I had to wear a foam neck brace for 8 weeks. (It was originally six weeks.) This was surgery number six, and I realized that the recovery doesn't always go as the doctors tell you. My neck surgery was 50% successful. I still had some of the issues I had prior to surgery, and I had some issues that I did not have before surgery, as well as severe pain in my hip. The recovery process was more than six weeks.

I returned to work after eight weeks, and I was on reduced workload for four hours. This did not last very long. My boss complained that my typing was very slow, and that I was not performing up to my original standards and the standards of my co-workers. Some of my co-workers thought I was "having my cake and eating it too," because I only worked for four hours and was getting full pay.

One co-worker made the comment, "You're so lucky!" On another occasion, someone said, "I wish I were you; you got it made." Finally, I said, "I would not wish what I'm going through, and still going through, on my worst enemy. Do you want to be in pain all the time? Do you want to be taking narcotics, like a drug addict, just so you can function?" Every day, I came home in tears because of the pain. The only way to cope was by taking one OxyContin three times a day for pain, just so I could go to work.

Every week, I would be in my doctor's office crying. I was trying to be a good wife, mother, friend, daughter, and co-worker. No one knew how much narcotics I was taking (except my doctor). I was doing a good job of hiding my pain from everyone, except my husband. He would see me crying every night but was helpless to do anything. For the next few years, it was a rollercoaster between work and disability, until I stopped fighting and went on long-term disability.

Two years later, I was diagnosed with Fibromyalgia, (please refer to chapter 9, pages 83-84 for more on this) which causes severe muscle pain, depression, insomnia, headaches, fatigue (never feel rested), memory issues, mood changes, sleep apnea, restless legs, and tingling in the hands and feet. I also had carpal tunnel syndrome in both hands, but more severe in the left hand. I was in severe pain and was unable to return to work. I was referred to Sunnybrook Pain Management Clinic. At the pain clinic, the pain specialist told me that fibromyalgia was "something doctors tell their patients they have when they don't know what is wrong with them." I was very shocked, so I did some research on my own. I went back to my family doctor and told him what the pain specialist had said. He was a little upset, but he told me that I needed to learn how to control this condition.

It was during this time that I realized my marriage was in trouble. I talked with my husband and asked him to go with me to marriage counselling. But he felt it was unnecessary, because everything was fine. I couldn't understand how two people could live together and basically live separate lives. But of course, he was living his single life; he would come home all hours of the morning, between 1 and 6 am, every day of the week. Someone introduced him to Bingo, and he would gamble away his pay cheques, which meant that it was left to me to pay bills. He never had money, and the bills were piling up. I was borrowing money from family and friends to make ends meet. When I had neck surgery in 1999, the same day I left the hospital, I had to go to a lawyer's office to declare bankruptcy. Then the bank foreclosed on our house and repossessed our car. I felt like I had reached rock bottom; there was only one way to go, with or without my husband.

It is impossible to fix problems in a marriage if only one spouse sees the problems. Over the years, I had heard rumors about other women. For three years, I tried to believe him when he said that people were lying, but it was obvious that they were not. I felt disrespected and humiliated.

I remember one incident where two women from my church asked me to go to another sister's house. Deep in my heart, I had an idea what they wanted to tell me. But I never imagined what would happen. I met a lady who told me that she had been having an affair with my husband for six months. She gave me a break down of their relationship: when, where, and how they had met. I was in shock, and I yelled at her that she was lying, but she knew a lot about him—except that he was married. She told a story of how someone had invited her to my church, and she started to come to lots of events. She was also studying the bible to become a member. She was at a church event at Thompson Park, and the person who had invited her was waiting with her and her children. Then her boyfriend came, and she introduced him to that person, who apparently knew him but couldn't remember how. A couple days later, she called her and told her that her boyfriend was married. She didn't believe it, so they set up this meeting to convince her.

My whole world had just come tumbling down! I didn't know if I should hate her or feel sorry for her that she had been duped. She had two kids and thought that she had found Mr. Right. I said she was stupid for not knowing he was married, but I was stupid too! The evidence had been there: the rose in his car that wasn't for me; the ladies' shoe that Natasha had found in his car, which wasn't my size; and him going outside or in the basement to make or receive a call. There were many more red flags, but I ignored them. I had lived blindly for six months. I was always suspicious of men, but I never thought that my husband would cheat on me. I always said that I would rather a man tell me the truth and then leave, instead of lying and being deceptive. My trust in men had just been destroyed, and I hated my husband for this humiliation I had just endured.

Of course, when I got home and told him what I had learned, he denied that he was having an affair with her. He said that she was dating his friend, so it was a case of mistaken identity. He went to the park for another reason and just happened to see her, and he offered to give her and her kids a ride home. I was so confused; I didn't know who to believe. I was angry at everyone and the way this was handled. I didn't need to see the woman; my friend should have told me the truth and asked if I wanted to go to the meeting. I was blindsided by people I trusted. He blamed the church for creating this drama, and he said that if we got separated or divorced, it would be the church's fault. He usually came to church for special occasions, like Christmas, Thanksgiving, Easter, or Natasha's recitals. He vowed not to ever step foot in the church again. I went to church a few times after this happened, but I didn't feel the same way. I was broken, and I couldn't handle seeing the other woman at church every Sunday. I was forced to make small talk with my husband's mistress. I decided to start going to a new place. I was told that she had stopped going to church too, for the same reason, and she was angry at me for doubting that she didn't know he was married. One year later, I started going to my old church again. They were my family, and they were always there no matter what I was going through.

One morning, in June 2001, I woke up and took a good look at my husband. He was fast asleep, still wearing his clothes from the previous night. He was so tired when he got home at 4:30 am that he didn't even get undressed. I was so tired from the night before; Natasha had been sick all night. She accidently ate peanuts (she had a food intolerance to peanuts, and the doctor said it could become a deadly allergy, so we should be very careful), which caused her to have major stomach pains, vomiting, and diarrhea. I lost count of the amount of times she vomited and went to the bathroom. She was so weak, I had to carry her from the bathroom to her bed. I was angry at my husband for not being home again. I was so scared. Here I was sick because I had recently had the RFA procedure, and I wasn't supposed to lift anything more than five pounds, and I had to lift Natasha and take her to bed. As I was crying in pain, scared and frustrated, I decided to call 911, and just then my husband came home. When he saw that I was awake, he was upset, because he thought I was waiting up for him. I told him about Natasha and suggested we take her to the hospital. But she started to improve; she was able to drink some water, and she slept almost the whole day and then was fine.

I felt like a single parent; my husband was never around, and we had been living on my income for a while now. I had been in the same job for twelve years, while he was not having much luck with his job. I made the decision that it was time for my husband and I to separate

As much as I still loved him, I did not want Natasha growing up thinking that this was how a marriage was supposed to be. My hope was to give him a reality check that he was going to lose his family, and that it would make him willing to make changes. I had always been a people pleaser, and I always worried about everyone else except myself. But now I decided that it was time to put myself first. After all, don't I deserve to be happy too?

I didn't leave my marriage right away; it took two more years and rumors of another affair that made me decide it was time to leave. I remembered the conversation that I had with my husband the night before. I told him that one day I would leave him, and he would come home and find the place empty. He said his favorite Jamaican slang: "You no have no sense." He never believed that I would seriously leave him. I packed up as much of my and Natasha's stuff and went to Suzette's house. I later arranged for the furniture and other stuff to be put into storage. Eventually, my family and N realized that I was serious, and I wasn't having a "temper tantrum." It became clear to

## The Miracle of God

me that leaving N had given him the freedom to feel justified to live a single life.

Some people very close to me did not support my decision. I was repeatedly told that I needed him because I was "sickly." Of course, everyone saw "poor sick Angela," "the sickly one" who needs to be taken care of. I had to prove to everyone that just because I had some chronic illnesses, it didn't mean that I couldn't be a good single mother. I knew that with God's help, nothing is impossible. ***"So do not fear, for I am with you; do not be dismayed, for I am your God. I will strengthen you and help you; I will uphold you with my righteous right hand."*** Isaiah 41:10

Being a single mom was not always easy, but I was determined not to let it negatively affect Natasha's quality of life that she was used to.

Ivita was such a good friend; whenever I had a problem, she was always there. We met while working at Miracle Mart, in 1984, and I know that God put her in my life for a reason. At that time, I was in my last year of high school. I was going to a private Catholic high school; there were 600 students, and only 20 were black. Ivita was my first black friend. I must confess that I didn't like her very much at first; she annoyed me. It seemed that we were always scheduled for the same shifts, so inevitably we became friends. She was a big help during this time. She went above and beyond what anyone could have expected.

My friend, Dawn, invited Natasha and I to move in with her and her family. I was the godmother to her two daughters, but I loved them like my own. Natasha was excited because there, she would be with her two sisters, and she would no longer be the only child. One morning while living with my friend and her family, I woke up to get ready to go to work (I was still on long-term disability but worked part-time), and I passed out. Natasha heard the noise as I hit the floor, and she found me. I did not realize at the time what a big impact this incident would have on Natasha. I was taken to the hospital and later diagnosed with deep vein thrombosis (DVT), a serious condition that occurs when a blood clot forms in a vein located deep inside your body. Because of the DVT, I developed a pulmonary embolism (PE), a blood clot that travels to the lungs, where it becomes lodged in a smaller lung artery. This could potentially be life threatening because it can prevent blood from reaching the lungs. Doctors said if Natasha had not heard me fall, I would probably have died, right there on the floor. Once again, God took care of me. ***"And the prayer offered in faith will make the sick person well; the Lord will raise them up." James 5:15***

    I made a pledge that I would make sure Natasha had a good relationship with her dad. I would not repeat what my mom did to me and Suzette. It was a lonely feeling to know that I had a dad that didn't really try to see his children. I often wondered if he thought about us; did he wonder if we had a place to live, food to eat, clothes on our backs? How can a man have only two children in this world and just not care? I just couldn't understand it, and I shed a lot of tears about it, but I couldn't change the situation. I wanted to co-parent with him and always do the best for Natasha. I know I went above and beyond to keep this pledge. From growing up until today, Natasha was a daddy's girl. Her first full sentence was, "Daddy good cook." She was convinced that I didn't know how to cook. I grew up in my grandmother's restaurant, and my mom let me cook at nine years old, and Suzette was ten years old, so of course, I can cook. She adores her dad and overlooks his flaws; in her eyes, he does no wrong! I used to get silently angry whenever she defended him. I would complain to Ivita when Natasha was not around. I did everything for her; I provided her with food, a roof over her head, clothes, and money when she wanted it, even if I had to borrow it. But she doesn't defend me; she expects so much more from me and gets upset when I say no, even though her dad says no all the time. I'm glad they have a good relationship even until now. Co-parenting is not easy, especially if there's anger and resentment, but as the law says, "We must do whatever is in the best interest of the child."

I had a lot of anger and resentment towards my husband. I felt like I was the victim and he was the villain. But with some coaching from members of my church, and some bible scriptures, I had to get some perspective. I know that all the problems in my marriage were not just my husband's fault. I must take responsibility too. There was a point in my marriage, after my neck surgery in 1999, where I pulled away from my husband. I was so consumed with taking care of Natasha, bills, work, and my constant health issues that we drifted away in two different directions. Like "two ships sailing in the night," the romance was non-existent, and we didn't make love very often. I was always in a lot of pain, and he was scared to even touch me. I wanted to make love with him, so sometimes I would try to hide my pain so that he would be more comfortable. I hated myself for not being enough for him, but I didn't know how to change the situation—this was my life.

We all endure heartbreak and tragedy; this is a part of life. How we react to it is what will show our weaknesses and strengths. Remember, God will never give us more than we can handle. Continue to the next chapter to read how God is testing our family.

# CHAPTER 5

# TRAGEDY

*"Blessed are those who mourn, for they will be comforted."*
**Matthew 5:4 (NIV)**

My stepdad was diagnosed with lung cancer. He had been a smoker for as long as I knew him, and he refused to stop. He was a man who never got sick—no flu, no cough, nothing. He would joke that whenever he got sick, it meant he was dying. He developed a cold, which got worse over a couple of weeks. My mom convinced him to go to the doctor because he had a bad cough and it wasn't going away. The doctor ordered a lung x-ray, which showed a mask over his lungs. A few days later, he went to the hospital to have a lung biopsy, which showed that he had lung cancer. He began to have chemotherapy and radiation. After a few months, he decided to stop the treatment. Six months later, he died. This was a difficult time for all of us, especially for my mom. They had been married for twenty-seven years, and now he was gone. My stepdad was not an overly affectionate man, but he did hug us if we hugged him. I don't remember him saying, "I love you," but he tried his best to provide for his family. I remember one Sunday morning when I woke up with the urge to go see him and my mom. I took Natasha with me; I didn't know that this would be the last day I would see him alive. I remembered that my mom had made him a nice plate of food, but he wouldn't eat it. We visited for a while and, as we were leaving, he gave me and Natasha a hug and said, "I love you." I cried at those words—I always felt that he loved me, but it was nice to hear it. A few days later, my mom called all of us to the hospital; he died in the middle of the night. It was devastating for all of us. I could hear myself repeating, "My daddy is gone; my daddy is gone!" He was the only dad I knew, and even though he wasn't my biological father, he was and always will be loved.

A few years later, my beloved sister, Kareena, passed away very suddenly at age thirty-four. It tore my heart to pieces. Kareena had mild cerebral palsy because she had been a preemie. My mom was only six months and two weeks pregnant when Kareena was born, and she only weighed two pounds, nine ounces. She was born in 1970, when technology wasn't like what we have today. The doctors had told my mom that she would not survive, but she proved them wrong. Kareena had cerebral palsy, which caused some physical and mental challenges. She had a learning disability, and mentally was a lot younger than her age. For example, even though she was thirty-four years old when she passed away, she had the mental capacity of a sixteen-year-old. She walked with a limp in her left leg and couldn't use her left hand; she was basically partially paralyzed on the left side of her body.

Kareena was the best of my siblings; I say this because she was sweet, bubbly, and very friendly. I remember, when she was a little girl, she would say "Hi!" to everyone she met. If we were in an elevator, she would greet everyone who came on the elevator, and say goodbye to them too. If they didn't answer, she would continue to repeat it until they responded. It would drive me and Suzette crazy! She would do the same if we were walking down the street. When we tried to explain about strangers, she couldn't grasp the concept. She loved to sing and dance; she had a great singing voice. She was the only one in our family who could "carry a tune." When we were all in elementary school, if Suzette and I saw a large crowd of children gathered in a large circle, nine times out of ten, Kareena was in the middle, singing and dancing. Some kids would ask her to sing and dance so that they could make fun of her, and that would be cruel.

But most of the kids truly enjoyed watching her perform. Kareena's favorite song was "One Day at a Time." When she sang this song, she would light up, and you knew she was singing from the heart.

One thing I must say is that she loved food. Her favorite was Kentucky Fried Chicken. At age 5, she ran away from her babysitter on two separate occasions. The first time she ran away, the police officer found her walking to KFC to buy lunch with her fake toy money. She got mad when they tried to take her home. Every Friday, we had KFC for dinner, which made Kareena very happy. She was also a big tattletale; she would tattletale everything we did and didn't do. My mom would always insist that we had to take Kareena along whenever we went anywhere. I remember one occasion when Suzette, Kareena, and I went to the store. Suzette was talking to a boy (which she wasn't allowed to do), so we bribed Kareena with candies not to tell my mom. When we got home, Kareena said, "Mom, I can't tell you why they gave me candies and told me not to tell you!" We can laugh about it now. Kareena was young at heart, always saw the best in people, and was much loved. I really miss her; she left an empty hole in my heart.

In May 2003, the company I was working for was sold, and my job was terminated. I was still on sick leave when this happened. It was devastating to work for a company for fourteen years, and all it boiled down to was a letter in the mail with a severance offer. The next day, I received my belongings by federal express, in a big box. That was it; I was no longer needed. It was a bittersweet moment for me: I was still in pain, so I couldn't return to work, but it had felt good to know I had a job to go back to. But that was not going to be, so first I got angry: "How dare they terminate me while I'm on sick leave; is that even legal?" I hired a lawyer and rejected the severance package. The lawyer was able to negotiate a disability and severance package that would help me until I was physically able to return to the working world.

Then I fell into a deep state of depression. I no longer had a career. This company had been my secure place for so many years. I also had friends there that I couldn't say goodbye to—I felt cheated! I barely left my house; I went out to take Natasha to school, or if I had a doctor's appointment, or sometimes to church service. I said "No!" to family engagements, church functions, and activities. My life had not gone according to my plan, but I was determined to bounce back and not give up. I had Natasha to think about, and I needed to stop feeling sorry for myself and step up. My mom always said, **"God helps those who help themselves."** I didn't know what my plan was, but I knew that God would lead me to the right path. ***"Trust in the LORD with all your heart and do not lean on your own understanding; in all your ways acknowledge him, and he will make straight your path."*** ESV

I realized that I didn't want to go back to another job right away. I didn't want to go back to the corporate rat race that had surprisingly made me happy for over 2 decades. I wanted to stay home and take care of Natasha and my health, but I needed to figure out what my next career would be.

For the next few years, I did volunteer work at Natasha's school. I helped with preparing healthy snacks, with pizza days, as a teacher's aide in the JK classroom, and I supervised the kids at lunchtime. I have always loved kids and really enjoyed being with them. Eventually, I started taking care of the kids after school, even some of Natasha's friends. This evolved into a home after-school program; at the same time, I began working as a lunch supervisor for the Durham District School Board, which I did for seven years.

In 2009 I enrolled in Early Childhood Education at Durham College. I knew that I couldn't go to school full-time with my unpredictable health situation, and take care of Natasha at the same time, so it made sense to do it online. Our lives seemed to be falling back in place. At sixteen, Natasha was an outgoing, happy, and healthy teenager. Her only complaint was having to work at McDonalds. I was taking classes, working part-time, and balancing my health conditions.

There were days when I was so exhausted that I couldn't get out of bed. I would have to call in sick. But thankfully, I had Natasha; she was a big help to me. I tried my best to do things myself; I didn't want Natasha to miss out on anything because of having to take care of me. My biggest fear was Natasha feeling like she got a "bad deal" having me as a mother. Someone once told me that I was selfish having a child with all my health issues. When she was younger, I would pray to God that I would live to see her 18$^{th}$ birthday. At that time she would be a strong and independent young woman. Now my prayer is I get to see her get married and have a child.

We were happy most of the time, but Natasha was still a typical teenager and tried to get away with stuff because I was sick and didn't notice—at least that is what she thought. I must admit that I spied on her, and I joined every social media site as soon as she joined them—MSN, Facebook, Instagram, and Twitter. I had to protect her; my job as a mother didn't disappear because I was sick. She called me a "stalker mom," but I was okay with that if I knew where she was safe. I should have known that my happiness wouldn't last forever!

One day after a routine physical examination, the doctor told me that I had too much protein in my urine, which is called *proteinuria* and is a sign of possible kidney disease. (please refer to chapter 9, pages 91-92 for more on this) I was recommended to a kidney specialist, who decided to do a biopsy. I was diagnosed with a rare kidney disease called IgA nephropathy (IgAN), also called Berger's disease. My kidney specialist was intrigued that someone could have so many different medical conditions at such a young age. He was convinced that I had a rare syndrome that would explain my medical history from birth to present. He was excited that I could be written up in medical journals. I did not share his excitement; I just wanted to be a normal mundane person and not have doctors look at me like they would love to dissect and study me. But anyway, normal was overrated. *"If you are always trying to be normal, you will never know how amazing you can be."*

He submitted a request for genetic testing at the Hospital for Sick Children. I was both excited and scared to receive the results. But unfortunately, after six months, the results were inconclusive. The reason was because they only had medical information from my mother's side of the family; they would need some information from my biological father's side. After years of trying to find out this information, I gave up the search—it became evident that this also died with him. I did extensive research over several months, with medical information from my family doctor, to see if I could figure out the syndrome I might have. I found out about Klippel Feil Syndrome and spoke to my doctors, who all agreed that my medical history does fit the symptoms of KFS, which can be associated with a wide variety of additional abnormalities that affect many different organ systems of the body. There are mild or lifelong cases of KFS, and it's obvious that mine is lifelong.

Having a diagnosis helps me to understand why I am the way I am. I felt good because I had a diagnosis, but bad because this syndrome could be passed to my grandchildren. I tried to find out as much as I could about KFS, and I joined an online support group for people with this syndrome. It felt good to talk with people who knew what I had been going through all my life. It was hard to hear the stories of children suffering from KFS at as young an age as two. I felt sad and heartbroken. I felt sorry for everyone with this illness, but I didn't get depressed. I wanted to continue living. I wished I could help find a cure for KFS, so that little children wouldn't suffer. I know that there are other severe illnesses that I can get from this syndrome, but I will not sit around waiting for them to catch up with me.

It was around 9:00 pm. It was a clear, dry night, and very mild. I was dropping someone home from a business event we had both attended. As I entered the intersection, I saw a vehicle coming from the opposite direction. She did not have her indicators on, so I assumed the car was going straight. As we proceeded through the intersection, she began to make a left turn without stopping.

Then she hit my car. It went spinning around twice and then smashed into the traffic post. The accident may only have lasted 30 seconds, but it totally changed my life forever. My first thought was to check on my passenger; she was screaming that she was having chest pains.

I reached for my phone to call 911, to get help for her. I was very concerned; I needed to get her some help. I called Natasha to let her know that I had been in an accident. I was in shock; I told her my car was in the traffic post. She asked where I was, and I told her the location; it was very close to our house. I accidently dropped my phone and lost the call. I couldn't get my phone. I began to assess the situation: My car was in the traffic post, and there were people banging on the window asking if we were okay. I realized that blood was coming from my mouth. I tried to open the door, but I couldn't open it. I was also unable to turn off the car. The paramedics and fire department arrived. They opened the door and they tried to attend to me, but I screamed for them to attend to my passenger. I thought she was having a heart attack. The other paramedics said that it was the seat belt squeezing her, not a heart attack.

They put a neck brace on me; then they took me out of the car, strapped me on a backboard, and put me in the ambulance. It was like a scene from a movie. I begged him to get my purse and phone so that I could call my daughter; she would be going frantic with worry. I was finally able to call Natasha, and I told her to meet me at the hospital. They put my passenger in the same ambulance as me and took us to the hospital.

Once we arrived at the hospital, I was put in a waiting area in the hallway for what seemed like hours. I was having a lot of pain; the back brace was uncomfortable, and the neck brace was very tight. I was wondering what happened to my passenger and was very anxious for the doctor to come so that I could get off this board. One of the paramedics came to see me; he said that he was leaving now, but he encouraged me to scream louder to get the nurse's and doctor's attention.

Natasha finally came, and I was so happy to see her. I could see that she was really panicked and had been crying. Once she saw me, she broke down in tears and kept asking if I was okay. I told her I was in a lot of pain and was feeling nauseous, so she ran to get a nurse. I was taken to get an x-ray of my neck. Around 1:00 am, the doctor came, and he said that my x-ray showed that everything was fine. He took off the neck brace and threw it into the trash can. Even though I was in severe pain, he didn't give me any medication. Natasha helped me get ready to leave; I was in so much pain, I couldn't do anything for myself. As we were leaving the room, Natasha suggested that I continue to wear a neck brace, and I agreed. I was in so much pain, and I was willing to try anything to relieve it.

Suzette arrived around 2:00 am, and she looked a little frantic. Natasha told me that she had called her. We saw the lady that was in my car, and her sister. Suzette went to speak to her, and they exchanged contact information. Then Suzette drove us home, saying that she would be back in a few hours.

The next day, Suzette took me to see my family physician. He was surprised at how I looked. I told him about the accident, and he said, "After all you've been through, you really didn't need to have a car accident." He wrote me a prescription for pain medication and gave me a note to take the rest of the week off work. A few hours later, Natasha contacted the daycare that I was working at to let them know

*Tragedy*

that I'd be off for the rest of the week. She also called the Toronto District School Board as well. (I didn't know it at the time, but I was never going to return to my jobs!)

What happened next was a surprise to everyone! Have you ever been misdiagnosed? Continue reading to find out what the big surprise was!

# CHAPTER 6

# MISDIAGNOSIS

*"I called on your name, L<small>ORD</small>,
from the depths of the pit.
You heard my plea: 'Do not close your ears
to my cry for relief.' You came near when I called you,
and you said, 'Do not fear.'"*
**Lamentations 3:55–57 (NIV)**

Day after day, I went to physio and massage therapy, but the pain was more severe after each visit. I was told that I had whiplash, which often takes a while to recover. I was in so much pain that when I got home, I would crawl up into a fetal position and cry. Natasha took the rest of her semester off school so that she could stay home and help me. I felt a little guilty about that, but there was so much I couldn't do myself. The days turned into weeks, and the weeks turned into months. I was still suffering with excruciating neck pain, headaches, sharp pain in the back of my head and ears, left shoulder pain, and it even hurt to chew. But worst of all was the sensation of electrical pulses on my head. I knew this was not normal, and not just ordinary whiplash.

I went to see my primary physician. Once I described my symptoms, especially the electrical pulses, he referred me to see a neurologist as soon as possible. I only waited a few days to see her because she had a cancellation. I was surprised that it was the same neurologist who had diagnosed me with Short Neck Syndrome over 15 years earlier, which led to my neck surgery in July 1999. After conducting her usual tests, she decided that I needed an MRI.

To my surprise, three days after the MRI, the neurologist called me. She said that I needed to go to the hospital as soon as possible. She told me that my neck was not stable, and she suggested that I go to the hospital and that I should take an overnight bag. I got off the phone feeling frantic; I wanted to cry but I needed to keep it together. I called Natasha, who had gone to the doctor. Her dad had driven her since we no longer had a car. I told her what the neurologist had said, and of course she had a lot of questions, but I didn't have the answers. She said that her dad would come and drive me to the hospital.

When I arrived at the hospital, I headed straight for the emergency department and gave them my name. I was told to have a seat. As I waited, I replayed the phone conversation that I had with the neurologist. She had said that my neck was not stable, and I wondered what that meant. I waited for what seemed like an eternity, but it was only ten minutes. I was taken to a room with a bed, and the nurse put a neck brace on my neck, without any explanations. She then told me to lie down on the bed. I was so bored that I decided to do a Sudoku puzzle while I was waiting. The nurse came in and, once again, she told me to lie down and rest. I suddenly remembered that I had forgotten my bag in the waiting area, so I went to get it and made a stop in the bathroom. When I got back to the room, the nurse looked a little rattled. "Where were you?" she asked me. I told her that I went to get my bag and had gone to the bathroom. She told me not to leave the room again, and that I could buzz the nurse for help if I needed anything.

About an hour later, a very handsome and young-looking doctor came into the room. I was very surprised that he was a neurosurgeon. He told me that I had broken my neck and needed surgery to repair the damage. He said that it was a miracle that I had survived for six months with this injury. I heard the same repeated from many doctors. I was told by one doctor that any wrong movement of my neck, like going to the hairdresser, could have been "lights out!" in his words.

They couldn't believe I had been having physio and massage therapy for six months. The surgery was scheduled for the next morning. He explained the possible complications of the surgery: becoming paralyzed from the neck down, losing my ability to talk, my voice could change, and of course, death. I felt scared, sad, and some despair. I cried for a few minutes and then I started to imagine how I was going to tell Natasha or my mother that I would be having major surgery. I decided to keep how risky the surgery was, and the possible outcomes and complications, to myself. I asked about not having the surgery, but he said that the outcomes could be the same or worse. I didn't see how it could get any worse, but I did sign the waiver form, stating that I understood the possible outcomes, and giving consent to the surgery. I tried not to think about the many things I had done over the last six months that could have been fatal. Natasha arrived a few hours later; she had a lot of questions, so I told her everything that the neurosurgeon had told me.

I didn't have surgery the next morning as originally planned. The neurosurgeon explained that I needed to be seen by a cardiologist to check my heart. I also needed to see an anesthesiologist who could give permission for me to be put to sleep. In total, I saw four doctors outside of the neurology field. The surgery date kept changing because they were having problems organizing the surgery with four doctors from different areas, to be available on the same day and at the same time. Finally, the operation was scheduled for June 13, 2013, four days after I had arrived at the hospital. I was terrified, but I knew that I needed to rely on God to get me through. I had many people at church praying for me and my recovery.

Suzette decided that we shouldn't tell our mom, because she

would be very worried. Natasha hadn't taken the news very well, so it seemed like a good idea at the time. However, Suzette's ex-husband told my stepbrother, who told my mom. She was very upset that we tried to keep it from her that I was going to have surgery. Amazingly, within 2 hours, she was at the hospital. She had taken a bus, subway, and walked, and she had gone to the wrong hospital. Luckily, they had a hospital shuttle bus that took her to the correct hospital. She was seventy-four and still going strong. The nurse told me that my mom came every morning at 8:00 am and left at 5 pm.

After the surgery, I was in an induced coma for two days. When I woke up, the neurosurgeon and a few interns and nurses were in the room. He explained that they were going to take out the tube, and that I should not attempt to talk. He also explained that if I couldn't breathe on my own, they would immediately put the tube back, which was very risky. I nodded that I understood. After the tube was taken out, I was unable to talk. I tried to write things down, but it looked like a toddler's scribbles. It was very frustrating not being able to communicate with people.

The next morning, I woke up tied to the bed rails. I asked the nurse why I was tied to the rails, and she began to tell me a story. She said that the previous night, at approximately 4:30 am, one of the night nurses came into the room and I was out of my bed and sitting in a chair. The nurse asked me to go back to bed but I refused; I kept asking for my mom and daughter, and saying that I needed to go to work. She tried to explain to me that it was 4:30 am, and that my mom and daughter had gone home to rest but would be back in a few hours. I still refused to get back into the bed. She called for a PSW to come in and help her get me back into the bed. Apparently, I attacked the nurse and fought with two male personal support workers before I finally got back into my bed. The nurse called Suzette and told her what had happened, and that I was a danger to myself and others, so she gave them permission to restrain me to the bed.

The head nurse arrived at 8:00 am, and she had been told what had happened the previous night. She came into my room and untied me from the bed. She was puzzled because during the days I was fine, and I didn't attack anyone. She called the pharmacist to check the medications, and it turned out that with the opioid medication that I was taking every night, I was incorrectly given two pills the previous night, instead of one, which explained why I was violent to the nurse and the two PSWs. I asked to see the nurse and the two PSWs when they came in for their next shift. I apologised to the nurse for scratching her and pulling off her ID necklace, which was broken. I was in shock when I saw the two male PSWs. They were both big, tall, strong men, about three times my size and body weight, yet I was able to fight them off before I could be put back into the bed. I also apologized to them, but they understood that it wasn't my fault.

It took a few days to get my voice and handwriting to come back to normal. I was wearing a neck brace, and I couldn't move my head or neck off the pillow at all; it felt so heavy and stiff. I was in the most excruciating pain that I've ever felt in my whole life, and I screamed so loud; I thought I would die! I couldn't do anything else but sleep. The nurse would come in every few hours and wake me up to ask if I was in pain. If I said yes, she would remind me that I had to push a button for the machine to send the medication to my intravenous (IV) and into my body. If I didn't do this regularly, they would take the machine away. She did push the button a few times for me when I was sleeping, but she wasn't really supposed to do that.

Every day, I had a lot of visitors from my church, my family, and friends. Sometimes there were lineups because I was only allowed two people in the room at the same time. The nurses sometimes made an exception to that rule. One week, in the intensive care unit (ICU), I received my custom-made body brace—it started at my chin and went down to my belly button. It was made of foam pieces and was very uncomfortable, itchy, and hot! I had to wear it every day except when having a shower; I had another brace for that. I was told that I had to wear it for three months, and I was not looking forward to it.

Most of the time that I was in intensive care, I had to eat soft foods, such as mashed potatoes, cream of wheat, jello, pudding, and pureed beans, chicken, beef, and pork. There was no salt or pepper in the food. It was very disgusting. I didn't like the pureed meat; it had a bad smell. Natasha started buying soup from the food court in the hospital, and Suzette would send me oatmeal porridge that she had made herself. Sometimes the food would be late, and then it would sit for a while until someone could feed me. I would be so hungry and anxious for the food, but once I saw it, I would lose my appetite. After my custom-made brace arrived, I could feed myself. One day, the nutritionist arrived, and she wanted to test if I could chew regular food. Once she was comfortable that I wouldn't choke, she gave permission for me to have some solid food.

After three weeks in the ICU, I was finally transferred to a regular room. The doctors wanted to send me to a rehabilitation hospital to help with my recuperation, but I was very desperate to go home. I was homesick, and I wanted my own bed, my cat, the freedom to move around, and to not be awakened in the middle of the night to have my blood pressure, temperature, etc. checked. They were concerned because I had lots of stairs in my house, which meant that I could easily fall. So, the doctor said that I could go home if I could prove that I could handle stairs. I said, "No problem; that will be easy!" In my head, I was praying to God that I could do it, because I wouldn't even be able to see my feet. The physiotherapist took me to the physio room and made me walk up and down some stairs a few times. The key was to hold the rail and walk slowly—I felt like a toddler being taught to walk again. I would also have to use a walker to help support my body. Finally, after three and a half weeks, I could leave the hospital. I was so happy to be going home. But I was aware that if things didn't work out at home, I would be going to a rehabilitation hospital for at least a month.

I was so happy to go home, and I was very anxious to see my cat, Jasmine. Natasha told me that Jasmine had been crying a lot and wasn't eating much, which was very unusual for her. But when I got home, she ignored me. I called her name and she just stared at me and walked away. I went straight upstairs to my bedroom to take a nap; I was already exhausted. While I was sleeping, I felt something heavy on my chest, and my face was wet. As I opened my eyes, I saw Jasmine sitting on my chest and licking my face. This brought tears to my eyes. I guess she was not expecting me to come back. From then on, my furry friend became my shadow, and a great companion.

I realized that the car accident had knocked me flat on my back. I had lost my dignity: I had to wear diapers, would poop on myself, and would have to be cleaned up by male and female PSWs. I was not in a race; I had no job to return to. Sometimes I wanted to be bitter and angry at God. I wanted to ask him, "Why me?" I saw everyone going about their daily lives, but I was stuck at home—and I was so envious.

I had an occupational therapist, and he was a godsend in my recovery. He hired personal support workers through agencies, and they came every day for three hours, to make my breakfast, give me a bath, comb my hair, and follow me to doctor's appointments when necessary. There were handrails installed in my bathroom, handles on the toilet, a bath bench, two walkers (one for each level), non-slip mats in the bathroom and kitchen, a hand reacher, a perching stool, hot and cold pads, a TENS machine, and special pillows. My house was transformed into my own rehabilitation center.

I had my first follow-up visit with the neurosurgeon, six weeks after leaving the hospital. I was using a walker to help support my body. After an MRI, I saw the doctor, and he told me that everything was going well, and that he was so happy with my progress. He also made a confession that he hadn't been sure of the outcome of my surgery—it had been a 50/50 chance of survival or success! I was very stunned by this revelation, since he had seemed so confident every time I saw him. He also said that I still had to wear the brace for another six weeks. I told him about the symptoms I was still having: I couldn't stand for long periods, and I had headaches, dizziness, and extremely painful neck pains. While I was wearing the brace, I still needed the PSWs to help me with bathing, combing my hair, a range of motion exercises, daily walks, and housekeeping.

I was counting down the days until my next appointment, when I could take off the brace and be free to move around. My house was becoming like my prison, since I couldn't go anywhere by myself. I would take short walks with the PSWs, but wearing the brace and using the walker made it very uncomfortable. Six weeks later, I saw the neurosurgeon again. I had a CT scan, and then he told me that everything was going as planned. So, I could take the brace off for 1 hour the next day, and one additional hour every day, until twenty-four days, which would be the last day. I was so excited that there was a light at the end of the tunnel. When the day came to take off the brace, it was the happiest day of that whole experience. I also graduated to using a cane instead of the walker.

I was still in need of help with everyday chores, like grocery shopping, and this was usually the task for Suzette and Natasha. I looked forward to these times because it gave me a break from the mundane days in the house. I knew that I was very lucky to have the help from my family, but sometimes I felt like a burden to them.

It was also boring and lonely at home. Now that I was home from the hospital, the visitors dwindled until there were next to no visitors at all. Everyone had their own lives. They go to work, school, parties, brunch, church, and out with friends, but I was trapped at home and couldn't go out by myself. I wanted the freedom to come and go as I wished. However, I did not complain, because this was how life worked, and I needed to focus on my recovery.

After two more months, I went back to see the neurosurgeon, without a walker or a cane. I had to have an x-ray this time, which was much easier since I didn't have the brace on. Once again, he said that everything was going well, but he was surprised and concerned that I wasn't using a walker or a cane. I told him that I had abandoned any walking aids, and I felt very stable and comfortable walking without them. He told me to be careful and that he would like me to use the cane a little longer. I continued to have six months of follow-up with the neurosurgeon, so that he could evaluate my progress and any problems I was having.

In May 2016, Ivita asked if Natasha and I wanted to go to Cuba with her and her family. There would be five of us: Ivita, Seth, Paul, Natasha, and me. It had been 25 years since I had been on a plane. I was a bit nervous but excited as well. At the airport, everyone had breakfast, except me. I had coffee and croissants; it was so early, and my stomach couldn't handle a big breakfast. On the plane, I wasn't feeling well, so I decided to use my inhaler. Natasha asked me what I was looking for. I told her that I was looking for my inhaler, so she took my bag to find the inhaler herself. I was getting a little annoyed with her bugging me, so I wanted to switch seats with Ivita or Paul. I stood up to talk with Ivita, who was sitting in front of me, and the next thing I remembered was waking up with Natasha, Ivita, a man, and a flight attendant around me, and I was wearing an oxygen mask. I asked Natasha what had happened, and she said that I had passed out. I heard Natasha telling someone that I had a heart condition, along with giving other medical information. I had to keep the mask on for the rest of the time on the plane.

When the plane arrived in Cuba, I heard the flight attendant telling everyone that there was a medical emergency that needed to be taken off the plane first. I asked Natasha what the medical emergency was, and she said, "You." I didn't think that my passing out was a big deal, but they insisted that I had to go to the hospital. I argued that it was unnecessary, but I had to go; they said it was airline policy. I did go to the hospital, but I signed myself out, and Natasha and I took a taxi to our resort. I was fine for the remainder of the trip.

When I returned to Canada, I went to my doctor. I told him what had happened on the plane to Cuba. He said that it was common, but because of my medical history, he would do some tests, and he referred me back to my cardiologist. The results found no medical reason for why I had passed out. It was probably because I took my medication without having a proper breakfast.

In early December 2016, I returned to see the neurosurgeon for my follow-up visit. After having a CT scan, I was able to see him. He was pleased with my progress; however, because of some symptoms I was having—twitches, headaches, tinnitus (ringing in my ears)—and because of the CT scan, he felt that I needed to have another surgery. I was a bit shocked, and I told him that I was not ready to have another surgery. He said that we could re-evaluate in one year, which would be July 2017. I didn't know it at the time, but I would never see the neurosurgeon in person again.

In thirty seconds, the accident had changed the course of my life forever. Continue reading to see how God gave me a second chance and a brighter future, which I never expected to happen.

## CHAPTER 7

## GOD'S PLAN

*"Trust in the L*ORD *with all your heart, and do not lean on your own understanding. In all your ways acknowledge him, and he will make straight your paths."*

When I look in the mirror, I see many scars—spiritual, emotional, and physical—that have shaped my life to this point. I know that my presence in this world was not an accident. God created me in his own image and likeness. **"I praise you because I am fearfully and wonderfully made; your works are wonderful, I know that full well."** My life is a miracle of God; for without him, I would not be here.

It's been over seven years since my surgery. I must live with not being able to move my neck. I have been especially careful because I know that my neck is almost completely fused! The doctor told me that there was nothing left to fuse in my neck. If I were to have another neck injury, it would leave me paralyzed or dead. Every day, I deal with some type of pain. Sometimes I can barely get out of bed. As a result of the accident and surgery, I have tendinitis in both shoulders, ringing in my ear, daily headaches, problems sleeping, and twitching.

It is very hard to explain how these symptoms affect my everyday life. My biggest loss is my independence to do what I want when I want to. I can no longer drive, but I do sometimes take the bus or the

## The Miracle of God

Go train on my own. But I'm terrified to take the subway on my own. I think about what would happen if someone were to push me a little too hard—the subway is extremely chaotic, with people rushing all the time. I must depend on others for a ride, or take Uber. I can no longer work with young children because it's too dangerous for me.

    I realize that it is difficult for people to understand what it's like for people with fibromyalgia, post-traumatic stress disorder, (please refer to chapter 9, pages 81-82 for more on this) and chronic pain syndrome, (please refer to chapter 9, pages 85-86 for more on this) and other illnesses. I have tried physiotherapy, massage therapy, TENS machine, acupuncture, guided meditation, yoga, psychotherapy, herbal treatments, and medical cannabis as well. I took the cannabis along with my other medications for two weeks. The doctor had told me to start with a low dose and to gradually increase it if I needed to for pain. While taking the cannabis, I felt that it was working to relieve my pain, but the side effect was that I kept passing out without any warning. There were a few mild incidents, but one was much worse: I was in the bathroom, sitting on the toilet, and I passed out and fell on the floor. I woke up with a big bump on my forehead, and my head was hurting and pounding. I pushed the Lifeline emergency button from the chain around my neck, and an emergency response operator asked me if I was okay. I told her what had happened, and she said that the fire department and ambulance was on its way. She told me to stay on the line with her until they arrived, but I hung up the phone. I went on my hands and knees because I needed to crawl from the third level to the second level in order to open the front door. The fire department arrived first and then the ambulance. One fireman asked if I was alone, and I replied that I was. Then he wanted to know who had opened the front door. I explained how I was able to open the door, and they said that it wasn't a good idea and that I should not do it again. Then I was taken to the hospital. I was lucky that I didn't have a concussion, but I still had a bad headache. They couldn't give me any more medication for the pain since I was already on a lot of pain medication already. I decided that it was best to stop taking cannabis because I didn't want to pass out again. So now I can only take my prescribed medication to deal with all my illnesses and pain. I tried a few times to stop taking some of the medication cold turkey, but on one occasion, I ended up in the hospital.

I've been dealing with health issues my whole life, and being the "sickly one" has held me back from many things, such as learning how to swim or to ride a bike, and it also made me an outcast in school. People didn't see me—*Angela*—I was invisible and hiding in the shadow of my sisters. Some of my parents' friends didn't even remember my name—they remembered Suzette's little sister, or Kareena's older sister, or Josephine's daughter. There was no doubt that Suzette was much liked by everyone; she had no problems making friends. Kareena was bubbly, had a sweet innocent face, and was always smiling, so I guess that describes it.

Of course, the middle-child syndrome—I was invisible. I had to *yell* to be heard, and I was described as boring, a bookworm, skinny, or sickly. My mom has baby pictures of everyone, except me. I once asked her why there were no baby pictures of me, and her answer was, "You were such a miserable baby, and you were always crying; no one wanted to take pictures of you." The earliest picture she had of me was my British passport as a two-year-old. From a kid to a teenager, I had very low self-esteem, and I was classified as a nerd. I used to bite my nails until they bled. Even though my fingers hurt and were so painful, it was a habit that took me a long time to break.

I'm so tired of the body pains, surgeries, medications, and the sometimes very painful tests. These have all been a part of my life for 55 years, and there has hardly ever been a break. I've learned to take things in stride, day by day, but I know there's no finish line—this is my life forever.

I have learnt that I don't have to live my life based on how people see me or expect me to behave. My health doesn't have to define me, but it shapes who I am today. I'm healthy in my mind and body, I'm loved, and I have a great family and friends who provide excellent support when I need them. My real-life experiences have helped me become a strong, courageous, competent, confident, and independent woman.

On August 23, 2019, Kevin, his sister, and I went to Florida for a week. We had a great time going to different outlet malls and shopping until we dropped. Kevin and I went to Universal Studios. I was so excited; I had always wanted to go to Disney World. We only went to one park, but it was amazing. On August 31, when we checked out of our hotel, I was not feeling very well, but I attributed it to the fact that we had woke up early to pack and be out of the room by 10:00 am. We had a long wait for our flight—11.5 hours to be exact. We had to decide what we were going to do to kill so many hours. We went to Denny's for breakfast, and then we went to Disney Springs. We did some window shopping and bought a few souvenirs. We decided to go to the movies because we still had a lot of time to kill. Kevin and I bought some food for lunch, and we ate while waiting for the movie to begin. I had to go to the bathroom, and I remember how laborious it was to go up those stairs to find Kevin and his sister back at our seats.

When the movie was over, I checked the Swoop app. "Good, our flight is on time," I told Kevin and his sister. The movie lasted about 2 hours, and then we decided to go to dinner. At dinner, Karen received an email from Swoop, informing us that our flight was going to be 1.5 hours late. I sighed—this was what we didn't want to happen. It was time to take the rental car back, and then take the shuttle to the airport. I was so tired; I felt like I had been hit by a truck. Since the night before, I had been having headaches and was having trouble breathing. I had been using my Ventolin a lot in the past few days. I was so worried that if we didn't get on a plane that day, we would be stuck in Florida indefinitely, due to the eminent threat of hurricane

## God's Plan

Darien. I was so worried that my inhaler and my other medication would run out. A few days before, I had called my pharmacy about getting the medication if we got stuck in Florida. She said that I would have to see a doctor, and it would be very expensive.

At the airport, we had to find a Swoop airline check-in. Of course, it had to be the farthest away. I didn't think I would have enough breath in me to walk so far, and I had to stop several times to catch my breath and use my inhaler. Once we were checked in, I was so relieved, but we had to walk to gate 92 to catch our plane. I sat down at gate 52 and made the decision that I couldn't go any further. Kevin's sister had gone to buy duty-free alcohol. Natasha called me, but I signalled to Kevin to answer it. He said that Natasha wanted to talk to me, so I took the phone and briefly explained how I was feeling. I had downplayed how bad I was feeling to Kevin and Natasha. When Kevin's sister came back, we all walked to gate 92. Kevin had to carry my bags. I was walking slower and slower and breathing very hard. I had to use my puffer twice again, and I had lost count of how many times I had used it that day, but I knew that it was more than the prescribed dose. But what else could I do? I didn't want to take the risk of having to go to the hospital. We were all elated when the plane arrived. It took another forty-five minutes before we took off. It had been thirteen and a half hours since we had checked out of our resort. I noticed that almost everyone was asleep, but I couldn't fall asleep, which was unusual for me. I was so happy when the plane landed at Pearson International Airport. I was so tired, and I could hardly wait to get to Ivita's house so that I could sleep. When we got off the plane, I could have cried when I saw how far we had to walk. Once again, Kevin carried my bags. I felt bad for him, but he assured me that he was okay.

Kevin drove me to Ivita's house at 3:00 am. We said goodbye and he headed home. A few hours later, at 8:00 am, my godson, Seth, woke me up. It felt like I had only slept for an hour, but it had been 4.5

hours. We had to get ready for my grandniece Yara's dedication. I was still very tired, and my breathing wasn't back to normal, but I didn't want to miss it. This was Leianne's (my niece) and her husband Leon's first child.

I was moving in slow motion, and my breathing wasn't back to normal. I used my puffers again and put them in my bag. Fast forward: Yara's dedication was very nice but late—the usual for my family. After the dedication, I was overwhelmed when I realized that I would have to climb a massive number of stairs to get outside. I barely made it to the car. We were going to the dedication after-party. All I can remember is getting into the car and closing my eyes. When I opened my eyes, there were people all around me. I couldn't understand what was going on, but I heard a voice say that she had called 911—I heard Natasha's voice, and others. I asked Natasha what was going on, and she said that I had passed out. I responded that I had just been sleeping. My words were slurred, and all I wanted to do was sleep. But a voice that I recognized as Sandra, my sister-in-law, said, "No, you can't sleep." The paramedics came, and they checked my blood pressure and glucose level, and both were at normal levels. They gave me oxygen and then decided that I needed to go to the hospital. I tried to explain that I was only tired, but no one would listen to me, so I closed my eyes and went back to sleep.

At the hospital, I was given oxygen and had a chest x-ray and ECG; then I slept as much as I could. After seven hours, they said that my oxygen level was back to a normal level, so I could go home. They told me to see my cardiologist and family doctor within one week—sooner rather than later. The next day, I received a voice message from the ER doctor, advising that I had fluid in my lungs, so I needed to get medical attention very soon. I found out that my family doctor was on vacation for two weeks, and the earliest cardiologist appointment I could get was three weeks away. I called the hospital and spoke to another ER doctor, who told me to come back to the hospital as soon as possible. I needed medical attention now, so I couldn't wait to see my own doctors.

Two days after I left the hospital, I was back again. They ordered a CT scan of my chest, and I waited for the results. About 1.5 hours later, the doctor said that I didn't have fluid in my lungs. Instead, I had pneumonia, and she saw something else on the image, so she said that she must talk with other colleagues. I wondered what she was talking about—did I have cancer? Needless to say, I was terrified. Pneumonia would be bad enough—and now cancer! For what seemed like a lifetime, she came back. She told me to wait a few minutes, and that another one of her colleagues would come and talk with me. Since I had already convinced myself that I had cancer, I was expecting an oncologist. Over the next 2 hours, I saw several different doctors, in different fields, but no oncologist. The last doctor I saw gave me a prescription for antibiotics and an additional asthma inhaler to use. He said that I had to come back in a few days to see an asthma specialist, but I could go home.

A few days later, I went to the asthma (please refer to chapter 9, pages 89-90 for more on this) clinic. The last few days were just a blur; all I did most of the day was sleep. I was very scared because asthma can be very serious. My sister, Kareena, had died from complications with her asthma and epilepsy.

At the hospital, I was directed to the pulmonary function test clinic, where I completed a series of breathing tests for over an hour. I was now waiting to see the doctor. I heard my name, so I followed the doctor to his office. For a few seconds, he was quiet while looking over my test results. He finally asked, "So, what brings you here today?" I responded, "I was sent here by doctors in the emergency department because I had passed out." He wanted to know what I thought the reason was that I had passed out on September 1st. I said that it was because I was exhausted from my trip to Florida, and that it had been a very long day before we got the flight home. For the next hour, he asked me endless questions about my health history, from birth until now. I began to give him a detailed medical history (in my head, I was wondering why he hadn't read my file before I got here, so that he wouldn't have to ask me so many questions).

The doctor delivered the BAD news: I had tracheomalacia, a very rare and serious lung condition, which could mean another surgery in the future. I felt like someone had hit me over the back of my head. The doctor was still talking, but I was still stuck on the word *SURGERY*. I was panicking in my head: "I can't do this again; I just can't do this again! Natasha would be devastated; she has put up with enough, with me and my health." The doctor said, "Mrs. Brown, do you have any questions?" "Ah, um, how did I get this condition?" He said that it was congenital, meaning that I had been born with it. I asked, "How is it possible that no other doctor saw this for 55 years?" He answered, "Other doctors were concerned with your heart, and they weren't looking for other issues. When your breathing and shortness of breath got bad, they diagnosed you with asthma, which you don't really have." I thought, "Wow, another misdiagnosis." I asked, "So, what's next?" The doctor said that there were two tests he needed to do to see inside my lungs. He would put me into a light sleep and put a tube down my mouth to my lungs, to see inside, and he would also take a sample of the tissue in my lungs, and have it tested. This was like a lung biopsy, except that he would flush my lungs with water to get his sample. Now came the question: "Could I have cancer?" He said, "It's possible but not likely; I'm looking for any infection in the lungs." This gets better and better! He scheduled the test for a week later. I would need someone to drive me home after the tests.

As soon as I got home, Natasha called, and I told her what the doctor had said. She was in shock! "How could you have this condition for 55 years, and no doctor figured it out!" I had the same question, but I didn't have the answer. So I turned to Google to get some answers. For the next few days, Natasha and I read everything we could about it, and about the tests I was going to have. A week later, Natasha took the day off, and she took me to the hospital and home again. Now all we could do was wait for the results.

Two days later, while I was having a nap, I got a call from a Toronto health nurse, from disease control and infectious diseases. She told me that the test results showed signs of Legionella, so I should see my doctor as soon as possible. She asked me a series of questions about my comings and goings over the last few weeks. She concluded that I most likely got Legionella from the resort in Florida, from the water when I showered. After the call, I thought, why me! Once again, I turned to Google, because I had no idea what Legionella was. My Google doctor told me that I had Legionnaires pneumonia; this was very serious and could cause death in one out of ten people who have it. Kevin and his sister didn't have any signs of the disease because they have a strong immune system, but I had a very compromised system from all my illnesses.

The next morning, I was up at 7 am, ready to see the doctor. The truth is, I hadn't got much sleep that night. My appointment was for 3 pm; I considered going to the hospital but decided to wait. After two and a half agonizing hours waiting, I saw my doctor. He checked the results and then gave me antibiotics. I told him what I had found out on Google. He advised me not to worry because my case was mild. I felt a little better as I went home. I called Natasha and told her what the doctor had said. As usual, she asked a million questions that I didn't have the answers to. It turned out that I had to take antibiotics for two weeks, to be sure that the disease was gone. Three weeks later, I had another lung CT scan. I went back to the asthma clinic to repeat the lung tests and a six-minute walk test. The results were good: The Legionella was gone, and my lungs were working much better. Thank God, another crisis was over. I had my flu and pneumonia shots, so I was ready for winter.

I'm sure you have realized that crisis will come and go, but you can always stay strong with God on your side. This is not the end of my story. I have a message I believe I was meant to share with you. Continue reading so you can learn about my message.

# CHAPTER 8

# MY MESSAGE

*"My mission in life is not merely to survive but to thrive; and to do so with some passion, some compassion, some humor, and some style."*
— Maya Angelou

**PART I: Thrive, Not Just Survive**

I love this quote by Maya Angelou. She stated clearly what I believe God has put me here to do. My message is that we must thrive, not just survive. But what does that mean?

**First, I need to live a life of purpose.** The car accident and subsequent surgery left me feeling isolated, very lonely, sad, and depressed. It felt like no one cared and that everyone had forgotten about me. I saw that everyone was living their lives—going to work, school, church, brunch, and parties—all except me. I felt lonely because there was no one around. After the car accident, I stopped socializing with my friends, family, and everyone. Once I was able to leave the house by myself, I didn't want to; I was scared. I had spent 4 months basically on my own for 14 or more hours a day. I didn't know how to be social, so I just retreated into my house. Going outside felt like such a burden and too much work. My house became my prison cell; I didn't make it a habit to go anywhere to interact with others. I needed to get out of my comfort zone. I realized that I was only surviving; I wasn't thriving. There was no purpose to my life, so I needed to make changes.

**Second, I needed to change my environment.** The first thing I needed to do was go to church. It felt so good to be in the fellowship and feel God's presence all around me. My church community really helped during my time in the hospital. Many people came up to hug me and welcome me back to church. I always knew that I had a lot of people who cared, and I still had a lot of friends and support. The Bible says, ***"And let us consider how to stir up one another to love and good works, not neglecting to meet together, as is the habit of some, but encouraging one another, and all the more as you see the Day drawing near."*** **Hebrews 10:24–25 ESV**

Once I went to church, it was easy to step up to the next level. I started going out for coffee, and sometimes for lunch or dinner with friends that I hadn't seen in a long time. I went to the gym, joined a yoga class, and joined a rotary club. I was starting the process of having a life of purpose and thriving.

**Third, I needed a new career path.** I could no longer return to my job as an Early Childhood Educator, because it was too dangerous to be around small children. My sister introduced me to her friend who is a financial advisor, and Natasha convinced me to resume my career as a financial advisor. I hadn't been in the business for thirteen years, but it was easy to pass the exams and get my license back. I was fired up! I went to lots of networking events, and I met lots of people. Some were in the financial fields, but the majority were digital marketers, coaches, bankers, realtors, etc. This gave me a whole new way of thinking. I knew that this was an opportunity to build positive, long-lasting relationships. And of course, making money was a good bonus too. This new career took me to places like Indianapolis and Las Vegas. I had expanded my horizons further than I ever imagined possible.

**Fourth, I needed to try something new.** My doctor recommended that I go to a pain clinic. The therapist at the clinic recommended that I take mindfulness meditation classes. I thought it was silly and stupid. I asked him, "How could meditation help relieve my pain?" I was upset because I misinterpreted the doctor's intent. I believed that he thought it was all in my head. It reminded me of when I was first diagnosed with fibromyalgia; a doctor had told me that fibromyalgia was not a real illness. He said that doctors only give this diagnosis when they don't know what's wrong with you. Of course, that was very upsetting. I decided to try mindfulness meditation classes; I was very surprised at how much fun it was, and it did relieve some of my pain. I took classes for four months until it became very costly. But I still do the meditations, along with yoga.

**Fifth, I needed to get rid of the negative voices in my head.** As a child, I always felt like an outcast, even in my own family. I felt so different from the rest of my family, not only in our physical appearances but our personalities too. The voices in my head wanted me to remain small. I once asked my mom if I was adopted or if she had kidnapped me. Of course, she said no. My mom didn't even have one baby picture of me, but she did of everyone else. Anyway, I convinced myself that I was a "fluke" of nature. I hated having my picture taken because I felt ugly. The accident didn't help my fragile self-esteem.

**Sixth, I needed to allow myself to enjoy life again.** I was allowing my illnesses to take over my life. Whatever you believe about yourself will be a reality. I needed to allow myself to enjoy the little things and be proud of myself for who I am. I knew that my negative thinking wouldn't go away overnight, but I took it slowly. I also voiced what I was feeling. It was good to have someone to talk to; online social groups were helpful and unbiased.

Since I now had more confidence in myself, I joined a dating service. This was one of the best decisions I had ever made. As you know, I met a wonderful man, and we have lots more adventures coming for our lives.

**Seventh, I needed to do things that made me feel good.** Doing things that make me feel good can have a positive effect on my life, my visions, and goals for myself. I needed to make myself a priority. I practiced self-care; I started to get my nails done once a month, and I got my hair done too. Meeting new people and having new experiences did make me feel good and positive about my life. I also enjoyed reading self-help books to find new perspectives.

**Eighth, I needed to ask for help.** I needed to realize that I was not alone. People wanted to help me, but I pushed them away. They didn't know how to help me. They knew I was suffering, but they felt powerless to help me, so I just started to ask. I talked with Ivita, because she knew me so well and saw me through many illnesses. I did speak to Natasha as well, but I didn't tell her everything. I spoke to a therapist; it felt good to talk to a professional and get some useful advice. I now have a good support network of friends and family when I need them.

**Ninth, I needed to love myself.** I used to ask myself: Why am I here? I didn't feel like I belonged anywhere. I blamed everyone else for my negative opinion of myself. I was bullied as a child, which made me feel ugly, worthless, and self-conscious of my body, especially my butt. I was constantly teased about "how such a small person could have a big butt." I thought I had put it in the past, but it was still holding me back. I tried to please everyone—my co-workers, my husband, my daughter, basically everyone around me. I thought this would make them like me and love me more. I thought if they were happy, then I would be happy. But deep down, I wasn't happy; I felt unimportant. But when I was living a life of purpose and focusing on myself, my thinking started to change. I must do what's best for me and what will make me happy.

**Tenth, I needed to make myself look good.** I decided to join a yoga studio, where I would go twice a week. They had classes of many different levels. This was very humbling for me because most of the people in that class were seniors. I didn't care because I was getting movement for my body and making connections. I took it slowly, one foot in front of the other. I learned how to do some of the simple positions, like child's pose, fetal pose, cat pose, and others. I also started to take short walks and use my treadmill. It was important that I liked how I looked; I was doing this for me. I also participated in a program called "Bye Bye Sugar." I never thought I could drink my coffee or tea, or eat my oatmeal, without sugar, but I'm doing it.

**Eleventh, my health doesn't have to define me.** It is obvious that I will never cure all my illnesses, and that I will have to live with them for the rest of my life. But I won't let that stop me from doing things I want to do in my life. I've been asked many times: "Why don't you just relax and stop doing so many things? Don't you realize you're sick?" My answer to these and similar questions is always the same: "I'm sick, not dead!" I have days when I can't get out of bed, and when this happens, I accept it and I stay in bed and take care of myself. But I won't stay in bed permanently.

**Twelfth, I'm not flawed.** I started to write a journal; I visualize where I want to be, what my short-term and long-term visions are, and I focus on who I want to become. I write positive affirmations that are specific to me. For example, "I am enough!" "I am special!" "I'm strong." I'm courageous." I can do anything!" Every day, I repeat the affirmations to myself in the mirror, and this helps me start my day in a positive way. Then I can deal with anything that comes along. I don't see myself as broken or flawed anymore, for the bible says, ***"You are altogether beautiful, my darling; there is no flaw in you."*** **Song of Songs 4:7**

**Thirteen, I'm a survivor!** My life is not based on how others see me. I'm healthy in my mind and body, I'm loved, and I have a great family and friends who provide excellent support when I need them. My real-life experiences have helped me become a strong, courageous, competent, confident, and independent woman.

**Fourteen, I listen to my body and my limitations.** My body has gone through a lot of changes— physically, emotionally, and mentally. It is important to not ignore these changes. I found that talking to a professional helped, and taking care of my needs, like getting enough sleep, eating healthy, and having no alcohol.

**Fifteenth, be invincible not invisible.** Regina Malabago says: *"You are bigger than your problem, stronger than your obstacles, and higher than your ego. You can make a difference; you are invincible."* Dream big, accomplish your goals and dreams, inspire others with your story, make a difference in someone's life, challenge yourself everyday, and don't make excuses—just do it.

**In order to move from surviving to thriving, there were a few important things to remember:**

**Change one thing at a time.** If I tried to change everything at once, I would fail. Then I would be back to where I began, feeling broken and alone.

**Be patient with yourself.** I was so excited about all the things I wanted to change, but sometimes they weren't successful. I must keep on trying. Never give up, and remember that God is in control. He wants me to succeed.

**Be patient with others.** Don't expect them to give you praise. Sometimes the people in my life did not react how I wanted them to— no "congratulations" or "good job." I would get frustrated and angry at them. They may have no idea why I'm upset, so I must wait for them to catch up.

*"As soon as you start to pursue a dream, your life wakes up and everything has meaning."* – Barbara Sher

## PART II: Follow Your Dreams

When I was younger, I wanted to be a teacher, a librarian, a housewife, a lawyer, and an author. My childlike mind thought I could be anything I wanted to be. Then I grew up, and I still wanted to be a teacher or a lawyer. Then I had a lot of excuses for why I couldn't follow my dreams—financial, time, laziness—all reasons that deterred me from going to university. So I went to college instead, and I didn't like the program(s) I took, so I eventually quit. But I do in some ways regret my decision. Why am I telling you this? Because now, at 55 years old, I'm fulfilling one of my dreams: I am becoming an author. You might say that I am already an author, with *The Courage to Change* book. But that was a *co-author*, which I'm also very proud to have been a part of.

You're probably asking yourself what's next once this is published. My goal with this book was to share my story so that people could see that even with many challenges in life, you can still overcome. I did not let my diagnoses keep me from getting married, having a child, or getting a divorce. I tackle one problem at a time, and I am patient with myself and others.

I would like to help women who have chronic illnesses, like myself, to achieve a better quality of life. I want them to know that their illnesses don't define them. There is a great life available for them; all they need do is step out of their comfort zone and try something new. Through programs that are fun, interactive, and creative, I can help them achieve their goals in life, like I did. My ability to be a part of a book project, and to write this book, is proof that it's never too late to achieve your dreams, no matter your age or medical status. I would also like to share my story on stages, and through podcasts, social media, and written articles, to help as many women as possible. I am determined to grow a coaching and speaking career based on my experiences.

When I think of the future, I think a lot about my mom and what her life used to be like. Now she has dementia, which leaves her with memory loss, confusion, anger, and reduced concentration. Suzette and, Miguel, I try to do our best to keep her comfortable and in her own place for as long as possible. I know she will get worse as time progresses, and the day will come for her to go into a nursing home. I fight back tears every time I think about it, but I will have to be strong when that time comes.

Sometimes our lives don't work out as we plan. There are so many moving parts of our lives, and things change so fast. One accident can change our lives forever. When the unexpected happens, we must do our best to overcome the challenges. Quitting at anything is not an option for me. Those who know me well, know that I always want to do my best, 110% of the time. There are times when I fail, but I get up again and keep going. There is no guarantee in life. I don't know if I may have more surgeries in my future (the thought scares me!), but if that happens, then I will have to deal with it.

I'm looking forward to the future, especially in my relationship with Kevin. This year, we will be going to Washington to meet his cousin and family. I can't wait for all that God has in store for me. This is my favorite scripture; it helps me to remember that God is always watching over me: *"For I know the plans I have for you, declares the Lord, plans to prosper you and not to harm you, plans to give you hope and a future."* **Jeremiah 29:11 (NIV)**

# CHAPTER 9

# RESOURCES

There were a few chronic illnesses mentioned in this book, which many people may not have known about. I want to give you some brief facts about each one.

**Post-traumatic stress disorder (PTSD)** is a type of anxiety disorder that is developed after someone has been involved in, or has witnessed, traumatic events.

**Causes:**

- Suicide in the family
- Car accident
- Domestic violence
- War
- Murder
- It can be caused by any event that makes you fear for your life.

**Symptoms:**

- Separation from others
- Flashbacks
- Nightmares
- Avoiding reminders
- Memory loss
- Using drugs or alcohol excessively

- Feeling jumpy
- Anger or irritability
- Depression

**Treatments:**

- Professional therapist
- Online support groups
- Medication
- In-person social groups
- Natural remedies
- Weighted blankets
- Something you enjoy doing (e.g., meditation, music, painting)
- Lean on family members or friends; they can listen.
- Write your triggers (e.g., sounds, smells, or objects) or flashbacks in a diary, so that you can learn to manage them.

**Common Myths:**

- PTSD disorder only affects Vets. **Fact:** It affects anyone, even children.
- People with PTSD are weak. **Fact:** Not everyone adjusts to traumatic events in the same way. Some people can't "just get over it!"
- Symptoms will surface right after the event. **Fact:** The symptoms usually develop within 3 months but can occur for years.

*Resources*

**Fibromyalgia syndrome (FMS or Fibro)** usually begins with different degrees of pain all over your body. There are specific pain spots that hurt when pressed with a finger. Pain spots are predictable, the tissue around the muscles or joints.

**Causes:**

- Domestic violence
- Genetics (causes increased risk)
- Emotional or physical trauma
- Being violently raped, kidnapped, attacked

**Symptoms:**

- Pain
- Fatigue
- Memory problems
- Anxiety
- Depression
- Sleep disturbances
- Headaches
- Numbness and tingling in hands, arms, feet, and legs

**Treatments:**

- Physiotherapy
- Self-care
- Medication
- Exercise
- Pain management
- Water therapy

**Common Myths:**

- Fibro is a psychological problem, not a real disease. **Fact:** It is a real physical disorder.
- Fibro is a diagnosis used by doctors when they can't figure out what's wrong with you. **Fact:** There is a specific set of diagnostic criteria used to diagnose FMS.
- Fibro is a middle-aged woman's disease. **Fact:** FMS affects men, women, and children of all ages.
- Exercise makes Fibro worse. **Fact:** When exercise is done properly, it can reduce some of the symptoms.

*Resources*

**Chronic pain syndrome (CPS)** is pain that lasts from three months to many years.

**Causes:**

- Osteoarthritis
- Rheumatoid arthritis
- Surgical pain
- Cancer
- Back pain
- Fibromyalgia

**Symptoms:**

- Sleep problems
- Depression
- Anxiety or irritability
- Joint or muscle pain
- Burning pain
- Fatigue

**Treatments:**

- Professional therapist
- Support groups
- Medication
- Natural remedies
- Physiotherapy
- Yoga
- Acupuncture

**Common Myths:**

- It's all in your head. **Fact:** It is a real disease, and it has clear biological traits.
- People with CPS don't look sick. **Fact:** There is no specific way that a sick person is supposed to look.
- CPS is caused by depression and anxiety. **Fact:** Depression and anxiety are common in many different diseases.
- Exercise can cure CPS. **Fact:** Exercise has been known to make CPS worse.

**Type 2 diabetes** is when the body does not process sugar correctly. A person's body may be resistant to insulin.

**Causes:**

- Combination of genetics and lifestyle choices
- Genetics: Hereditary, race, and ethnicity
- Lifestyle choices: Lack of exercise, unhealthy eating (high fat and/or low fiber diet), overweight or obese

**Symptoms:**

- Fatigue
- Increased urination
- Increased hunger
- Increased thirst
- Losing weight
- Wounds taking too long to heal
- Blurred vision

**Treatments:**

- Medication
- Natural remedies
- Healthy eating
- Maintaining healthy weight
- Medication or insulin
- Exercise

**Common Myths:**

- People with diabetes can't eat sugar. **Fact:** People with diabetes need a balanced diet, which includes sugar.
- Type 2 diabetes is mild. **Fact:** There is no mild form. If not managed well, it could lead to life-threatening conditions.
- Type 2 diabetes only affects fat people. **Fact:** 20% of people with type 2 diabetes are normal or underweight.
- People with type 2 diabetes should only eat *diabetic* foods. **Fact:** *Diabetic* foods can cause problems, so don't eat them.
- People with diabetes go blind or lose their legs. **Fact:** People with diabetes don't go blind or lose their legs if they have a yearly diabetes health check-up.

*Resources*

**Asthma** is a chronic lung condition. The breathing tubes can swell and constrict, causing asthma symptoms. The airway gets inflamed and narrow, making breathing difficult.

**Causes:**

- Allergies: animal dander, weed pollen, trees, grass, molds, and dust mites
- Food and food additives
- Exercise
- Heartburn
- Smoking
- Medications
- Weather
- Smoke
- Sinusitis

**Symptoms:**

- Tired, easily upset, grouchy or moody
- Losing breath or having shortness of breath
- Frequent coughing, especially at night
- Wheezing or coughing after exercising
- Chest tightness, pain, or pressure

**Treatments:**

- Medication: quick and long-term relief
- Rescue inhalers
- Maintain healthy weight
- Medication
- Exercise
- Avoid triggers

*The Miracle of God*

**Common Myths:**

- People with asthma can't exercise. **Fact:** Exercise is okay if asthma is controlled.
- People will outgrow asthma. **Fact:** Asthma cannot be outgrown.
- Nobody dies from asthma. **Fact:** There's a real risk of dying if asthma is not controlled.
- Asthma medications are habit forming and dangerous. **Fact:** Asthma medications are not habit forming; they're not like opioids.
- Chihuahuas can cure my child's asthma. **Fact:** They cannot cure asthma.

*Resources*

**Kidney disease** is the gradual loss of function of one or both kidneys.

**Causes:**

- High blood pressure
- Diabetes
- Autoimmune diseases
- Overuse of some medications
- Heart disease
- Family history of kidney failure

**Symptoms:**

- Fatigue or weakness
- Change in urination
- Loss of appetite or losing weight
- Itchy skin
- Swelling in the legs, feet, and/or ankles
- Muscle twitches and cramps
- Dizziness or decreased mental focus
- Shortness of breath

**Treatments:**

- Medication to reduce blood pressure and cholesterol, or to protect bones
- Healthy eating (reduce salt and protein intake)
- Maintain a healthy weight
- Dialysis or kidney transplant for advanced cases

**Common Myths:**

- Kidney disease is rare. **Fact:** It is a very common disease.
- If I have it, I will know. **Fact:** Many people have it and don't know.
- Testing is long and expensive. **Fact:** Testing is easy with a urine or blood test.
- If the person is at risk, nothing can be done. **Fact:** Not everyone who is at risk will get it. Many things can be done to prevent it: eat healthy, exercise, don't smoke, control blood pressure and blood sugar.
- No one knows what causes kidney disease. **Fact:** A common cause is diabetes and high blood pressure.
- The only treatment is dialysis. **Fact:** Kidney disease is progressive. An early stage can be managed with exercise, diet, and medication.

# Work Cited Page

### ASTHMA

"Asthma Symptoms and Signs."
www.webmd.com/asthma/asthma-symptoms#1

"Common Myths about Asthma"
www.health.usnews.com/health-care/for-better/articles/2018-12-04/common-myths-about-asthma

"What Causes Asthma? Common Triggers Explained."
www.webmd.com/asthma/asthma-triggers#1

"Asthma MythBusters" ,https://health.usnews.com/health-care/for-better/articles/2018-12-04/common-myths-about-asthma

### CHRONIC PAIN SYNDROME

"What Is Chronic Pain Syndrome."
www.healthline.com/health/chronic-pain-syndrome

### DIABETES

"Type 2 Diabetes Symptoms and Early Warning Signs.",
www.endocrineweb.com/conditions/type-2-diabetes/type-2-diabetes-symptoms

"Diabetes Myths."
www.diabetes.co.uk/diabetes-myths.html

## FIBROMYALGIA

"Fibromyalgia Symptoms."
www.webmd.com/fibromyalgia/guide/fibromyalgia-symptoms#1

"Fibromyalgia Myths and Facts."
www.prohealth.com/library/evergreen_pages/fibromyalgia-myths-and-facts

## KIDNEY DISEASE

"Myths about Kidney Disease."
https://www.kidney.org/newsletter/six-common-myths-about-kidney-disease

"Myths about Kidney Disease"
https:/www.kidney.org/news/kidneyCare/winter10/MythsAboutKD

"Types of Kidney Disease"
https://healthprep.com/kidney-liver/types-kidney-disease

## POST TRAMATIC STRESS DISORDER

"Symptoms of PTSD."
Mind, www.mind.org.uk/information-support/types-of-mental-health-problems/post-traumatic-stress-disorder-ptsd/symptoms-of-ptsd/#b.

"10 Symptoms of PTSD."
www.facty.com/conditions/ptsd/10-symptoms-of-ptsd/

"5 Myths about PTSD."
www.psychologytoday.com/ca/blog/the-truisms-wellness/201610/5-myths-about-ptsd

www.ingramcontent.com/pod-product-compliance
Lightning Source LLC
LaVergne TN
LVHW051507070426
835507LV00022B/2973